ADVAN

Freirea

Scholars and Pr... Dialogue on Critical Ideas in Education

"Truth be told, Freirean education is more necessary now than it has ever been. As a critical contemplation for educators to consider when re-imagining, implementing, and evaluating Freirean foundations during these unprecedented times, *Freirean Echoes: Scholars and Practitioners Dialogue on Critical Ideas in Education* offers contemporary, liberatory, and powerful insights that aim to uplift ideas that might otherwise be silenced by mainstream approaches to reform. This is a must-read anthology for educators and those concerned with humanization and social transformation in society and schools."

—Patrick Camangian, Professor of Teacher Education
University of San Francisco

"This stunning, intergenerational volume of speeches, inspiring vignettes and brilliantly framed questions is perfectly timed for us to celebrate Paulo Freire's centennial year and to reflectively renew the challenge his life brings to our own praxis. Indeed, this collection lovingly compels us to share Freire's rare and precious gift of vision that critically views and denounces oppression while inspiring us to continually see and declare the possibilities of freedom for all people. These two aspects of critical consciousness can be metaphorically compared to our physical capacity of sight which holistically unites the field of vision in both eyes into one unified perspective."

—Robert Lake, Professor of Social Foundations and Curriculum Studies
Georgia Southern University

"*Freirean Echoes: Scholars and Practitioners Dialogue on Critical Ideas in Education* is a magnificent book that expands the boundaries of critical pedagogy. As readers enter the dialogic space created between scholars and educators of past and present, they'll be challenged to reflect on the power and possibility of Paolo Freire's vision coming to life. Each chapter inspires a sense of renewal and hope that being human means recognizing that we are unfinished. This collection of essays thoughtfully celebrates what happens when distinguished authors and inquisitive readers share space reimagining education, community, and the world."

—Christopher Lewis, Freirian scholar and K-12school practitioner
in the El Monte Union High School District

Freirean Echoes

Myers Education Press

Published by Myers Education Press, LLC
P.O. Box 424 Gorham, ME 04038

Myers Education Press is an academic publisher specializing in books, e-books, and digital content in the field of education. All of our books are subjected to a rigorous peer review process and produced in compliance with the standards of the Council on Library and Information Resources.

Library of Congress Cataloging-in-Publication Data available from Library of Congress.

13-digit ISBN 978-1-9755-0495-3 (paperback)
13-digit ISBN 978-1-9755-0496-0 (library networkable e-edition)
13-digit ISBN 978-1-9755-0497-7 (consumer e-edition)

Printed in the United States of America.

All first editions printed on acid-free paper that meets the American National Standards Institute Z39-48 standard.

Cover design by Teresa Lagrange

Image design by Claudette Judes

Freirean Echoes

Scholars and Practitioners Dialogue on Critical Ideas in Education

Edited by
Charlotte Achieng-Evensen
Kevin Stockbridge
and
Suzanne SooHoo

Myers Education Press
GORHAM, MAINE

CONTENTS

Section Five

DEDICATION TO TOM WILSON

SUZANNE SOOHOO

Context

The editors wish to dedicate this book to Dr. Tom Wilson, who passed away on December 28, 2018. He was the founder and moral spine of the Paulo Freire Democratic Project. Without him there would be no Freire at Chapman University. He leaves a treasured legacy, but what is more important than what he did is who he was—an ethical, insightful, joyful human being.

Suzanne SooHoo, co-director of the PFDP and loyal friend, described her professional relationship and special friendship with Tom at his Celebration of Life on March 28, 2019, at Chapman University.

Memories of Tom Wilson: Celebration of Life

Dr. Tom Wilson founded the Paulo Freire Democratic Project (PFDP) in 1996. The (PFDP) is a collection of local, regional, and international initiatives headquartered in Chapman University's Donna Ford Attallah College of Education Studies. These initiatives reflect the political, pedagogical, and ethical imperatives of the great Brazilian educator Paulo Freire and capture his democratic struggle for social justice.

Tom was a personal friend of Paulo's and, after a handshake agreement in 1995, they agreed that the PFDP would be established in southern California at Chapman University. Prior to the establishment of the PFDP, Tom was a member of a group initiated by Suzanne SooHoo, the Collaborative Action Researchers for Democratic Communities. Shortly after Paulo's blessing, the group agreed to rename itself the Paulo Freire Democratic Project.

Fond Memories of Tom Wilson

I first met Tom 30 years ago when I was an elementary school principal at a conference convened by UCLA's John Goodlad, known for his work in *A Study of Schooling*. At that time I also met Ken and Barbara Tye, founding deans of the Department of Education at Chapman University, who were also part of the famous Goodlad research team. As a young principal striving to be a visionary progressive educator, I was intrigued with the opening activity in Tom's workshop. He asked us to think for a moment and erase all notions of schooling, to figuratively burn the schools down as we know them. Then, on butcher paper and with crayons, to imagine and draw the ideal school—the classrooms, students, teachers, teaching and learning. I thought to myself, was this treason or a strategy to unlock the brain with shock and awe?

Our relationship developed from that point on, as Tom was invited to be a critical friend to me, my school, and a group of teacher researchers. These teachers—the Teacher Researchers for Democratic Communities (Susie Weston, Chris Byron, Lani Martin, Cheryl King, and Emily Wolk)—were the forerunners of the PFDP. When I left the principalship in 1991, Tom and I worked at UCI as co-directors of school–university partnerships, and later Tom joined me at Chapman University as coordinator of the Master of Arts in Education program. Tom and I co-taught classes in critical pedagogy and social justice. We have traveled together to various AERA conferences and also to Russia to speak on democracy in the classroom. We reasoned that "No one in America has invited us to have a conversation about democratic classrooms, so why not Russia?" Traveling was routinely problematic because Tom's name was on a federal watch list as a result of being a conscientious objector to the Vietnam War. He was always asked to step out of line at the airport, and not until many years later did this situation get resolved, but it took an act of Congress (a congressman's letter) to resolve Tom's status.

Upon our arrival in Russia, we were informed that there would be no hot water. We reasoned that we could wait a couple of days, but then they told us there was to be no hot water for the whole summer! We were nearly removed from the sleeper train in the middle of the night for refusing to pay $1.50 extra for the sheets and towels, which—in rubles—appeared to amount to thousands of dollars. We had been told by Russian colleagues to beware of people taking advantage of Americans, and we were suspicious of the train staff. We had to gift the conductor several bottles of vodka to regain his good graces in order to be allowed allow to stay on the train.

Soup, Cookies, Fried Eggs

Tom loved soup, whether it was cocky leaky soup at Rutabegorz restaurant, or borscht in Russia. Because soup was his meal of choice, he maintained that svelte body by running marathons and working out every day.

He was a faithful morning runner, even in chilly AERA cities like New York and Chicago. Tom beat everyone in his age group because there were few or no competitors.

Tom could smell a cookie three buildings away. If you ever wondered who stole the cookies from the cookie jar, your best bet was Tom. At two o'clock every day at UCI, Tom and I would hunt for a cookie, sometimes dropping by the food table for a reception we weren't invited to. If we couldn't find a cookie, we'd buy one at a kiosk, and Tom would inevitably ask me to put it on his tab because he didn't carry cash. I was the cookie enabler, as he ran a monthly $50 tab! He said cookies fed our souls. At his UCI retirement party, we enjoyed an international collection of beer and munched on cookies.

When Paulo would come to southern California to visit Claremont, UCI, or Chapman, Tom was his reliable host. Tom and he would take drives in Tom's Mercedes and dine at Felix's Cuban Café in the Orange circle. I recall Paulo ordering beans and rice and requesting that a fried egg be placed over it that wasn't on the menu. The waiter informed us that the restaurant stopped serving eggs at breakfast, to which Paulo responded, "This is America; why would an egg be available only in the morning?" He eventually got his egg, as no one could find a reason to deny his request. Paulo claimed you could never trust anyone if they didn't eat and drink heartily. Tom also believed that there was a relationship between eating and building friendships. He remembered his father's quip, "You can call me anything—just don't call me late for dinner."

As a Teacher

Paulo: "If the structure does not permit dialogue, the structure must be changed."

We co-taught many classes together. Tom approached classes not as one who knows everything but as one who questioned everything. In his Democracy and Education course, he routinely began with no syllabus and a question for the students: What did they want to study and learn? He asked them to fill in the blank syllabus. Some eagerly took advantage of the invitation, but most were suspicious and cautious. When he reassured them of his earnestness, they became angry, proclaiming that it was his job to create a syllabus. He was the expert. Why would he waste their time with this silly exercise, claiming they didn't know what they should be learning? A few students made appointments with the dean to file a complaint. After a couple of weeks, the initial chaos would dissipate, and Tom would respond to students' frustrations with questions: Why do you assume I am "the expert?" Why, as graduate students, do you not know what you want to learn? What expectations did you have about schooling, and where did those notions come from? These questions launched the semester's work of critical pedagogy with students who were well schooled but poorly educated.

As a Fellow Faculty Member

Administrators and friends such as Don Cardinal would comment that Tom often was misinterpreted; he needed translation, which Don skillfully navigated. Vice Chancellor Manual Gomez of UCI lovingly referred to Tom as a philosophical gnat, as Tom would buzz and bite into his administrative consciousness. Barbara admired and appreciated how Tom would call attention to the moral and ethical implications of our faculty decision-making by asking, "Wait a minute, what are we saying here?"

As an Intellectual

John Dewey, Lawrence Kohlberg, John Rawls, Chris Agyris, and Paulo Freire were among the many scholars who informed Tom's sense of justice. He found daily examples of Agyris's espoused theory and theory-in-use. He incorporated John Rawls's social contract activities by asking students, "What is a fair way to cut a cake?" and inviting them to design a fair and just society.

One of his favorite pastimes at AERA conferences was to visit progressive schools like Central Park East and the Peace and Freedom School in New York. He particularly liked meeting up with Richard Hayes, a fellow Kohlbergian, wearing a hat he designed for the both of them that read "Larry 7."

Tom was the person you would approach to get clarity on issues. His furled brow and careful listening made you feel you were the only person in the room or on the phone. And when we failed, Tom would ask, "What is the worst that could happen? Will they fire you? You are not really an activist unless you have been fired a few times." He would reassure us to alleviate our trepidation, while also explaining his uneven career record. His underlying moral questions—"What would you do to remain free? What would you risk in the name of democracy?"—replaced our helplessness with newfound courage.

Wording

Tom, like Paulo, had faith in human beings' ability to solve both individual and social problems through dialogue and critical consciousness. On his kitchen mantle he had critters arranged in a cultural circle: a dog, Winnie the Pooh, a penguin, a dolphin, a dinosaur, and a turtle. His belief in the power of collective consciousness informed his dialogical compositions and his affection for fellow human beings.

Tom, again like Paulo, was keenly interested in the etymology of words—words and their origins and accompanying histories. His favorite lifelong research project was to evaluate how often the words democracy, freedom, and equity came up in speeches or essays. Back in the mid 1990s, he collected sets of papers from Russian and U.S. high school students, and his preliminary findings showed that Russian students contemplated democracy more than students from the United States. When *wordle* became popular, he waxed ecstatic as he filtered every political essay he could get his hands on for keywords. Remember the key words word wall we constructed at AERA to celebrate an anniversary of Paulo's work ten years ago?—endless sheets of butcher paper sprawled across ballroom floors; students and scholars on their knees, fannies in the air, drawing critical words and cartoons. This was a novel experience for all, including our discussants Peter McLaren and Maxine Greene, who were amused by how Tom orchestrated this atypical AERA activity.

Another example of Tom's wordplay can be found in his chapter "Learning Moments" in Sonia Nieto's 2008 book, *Dear Paulo*, which includes an anagram tribute to Paulo: P: partying with passion; A: attending; U: undercutting, unflinching, unrelenting; L: loving; O: obligating. Tom ended the chapter with a note: "my obligation to myself and to your memory."

When I told him my primary language was a language of silence that came from my father, who advised, "Don't say anything unless you can improve upon the silence," he was charmed, and he reminded me that it was my responsibility to communicate with words to others. Likewise, I reminded him that communication was a mutual responsibility and invited him to learn my wordless language. We spoke many languages to each other—language of respect, words of collegiality, expressions of love for humanity. I will also miss his disquieting insights.

Humility

Tom was exceptional in that he did not aspire to be exceptional. He was a humble person. He chose to be everyday regular, ostensibly simple, pragmatic, and loving. His independent nature allowed him to be free of careerism, publication deadlines, or the shackles of promotion and tenure, because he judged his self-worth with a different metric: consciousness-awakening teacher; ethical, compassionate human being; and informed, responsible citizen of the world. He contested the *banking model* of education, but he believed in *investing* in future generations as he helped young people discover multiple possibilities for themselves in this ever-changing world.

Dreaming

Tom recognized that the dynamic quality of consciousness involved dreaming the unimaginable. He spent almost his entire lifetime daring to dream a democratic model school in La Escuela Freire. Like a master craftsman, he would read or experience something profound and then rush to apply it in his literary painting, carefully adding new strokes to his dreamscape canvas. He loved sharing this passion with others and was eager to talk about its current evolution. It was his way of testing these ideas for their democratic strength and their capacity to serve the common good. While Tom is no longer physically with us, his absence does not diminish the power of his ideas.

Advising

Tom and I enjoyed sitting in his back garden patio, where a vibrant bougainvillea tree generously draped itself over the back fence. The brilliant magenta tissue-paper flowers commanded attention. You could not take your gaze off of them. It was an ideal reflection point to think about life.

Suzi: "Retirement makes one contemplate mortality. What is my purpose now that I'm retired?" I asked, as I maintained my gaze on the bougainvillea flowers, as if they had the answer for me.

Tom: "Just enjoy and follow your heart. The bougainvillea has no purpose except to be."

Suzi: "But I have always existed for a purpose. I know little about just *being*. How do I replace purpose with *being*?"

Tom: "Then that becomes your new purpose."

Remembering

"I can't remember things anymore," he complained. Heart remains while mind is failing. No longer the battle between heart and mind. Memory failure prepares you to lead with your heart. I assured him that while his memory was fading, our memories of him are not lost. I reminded him how they are captured in this upcoming book and future video project. Hundreds of students stand on his shoulders; their lives continue to be informed by his wisdom. And dear friend, there is not a class or a lecture I give that does not evoke your spirit.

Resisting

At our last visit together in November 2018, Tom was reading a book on *Fascism* that chronicled how Trump had amputated multiple forms of democracy and cannibalized the human spirit of at least half the nation in his two years in office. A careful examination of Tom's margin notes will tell us what filled his thoughts in his last weeks.

He has always been enamored with the 1960s and students' willful dissent and courage to talk back. When asked how the read was, Tom replied, "I don't do much these days except occasionally give Trump the finger." This was one of Tom's last willful acts of resistance, a fearless gesture to keep us free.

Standing

Regardless of one's faith, heaven must be beautiful with Tom engaged in dialogue, conversation, and problem-posing with new and old friends. If we believe in reincarnation, look for Tom every time someone poses a question about equity and fairness, or someone who lovingly scratches the ears of a golden retriever or listens to the wind that carries Tom's wisdom and love. I know I will, because he is the reason I AM, and, for the Paulo Freire Democratic Project, the reason WE ARE. We love you Tom!

Reference

Nieto, S. (2008). *Dear Paulo*. Taylor and Francis.

ACKNOWLEDGMENTS

We wish to thank . . .

Paulo Freire Democratic Project at Chapman University and the contributing authors of this book, for their communal solidarity.

Donaldo Macedo, for inspiring us to produce a book capturing keynote speeches, thus extending their immortality.

Chris Myers, who supported the idea of a book about dialogue to add to Myers Education Press's niche collection for Freirean scholars.

Patrick SooHoo, for his cover design research, translating words into compelling images.

Jean Wilson, life partner of Tom Wilson, who gave us permission to use SooHoo's *Life Memorial Speech to Tom Wilson* as a book dedication to our dearest friend Tom Wilson. We envision Tom and Paulo having an afterlife dialogue and together enjoying Tom's favorite snack, a cookie.

INTRODUCTION

Can Text Be Dialogic? An Introduction

CHARLOTTE ACHIENG-EVENSEN, KEVIN STOCKBRIDGE, AND SUZANNE SOOHOO

WHY DO MOST BOOKS begin without the ritual of an opening greeting? What does that type of start suggest? Such books appear to have a bold "Here I Am" confidence announcing their existence, independent of human engagement. At first glance, books of this type are typically non-transactional, seemingly disinterested about the person who picks them up.

We start this book with different assumptions. In one of many attempts to humanize our everyday existence, we begin with an invitation to you, asking you to engage in mental dialogue with us. We welcome you in, asking that you join us in an ensuing conversation among authors who are collectively echoing Paulo Freire.

> "Really reading involves a kind of relationship with the text, which offers itself to me and to which I give myself and through the fundamental comprehension of which I undergo the process of becoming a subject." (Freire, 1998, p. 34)

Reading, according to Freire, involves a kind of active intimacy cultivated among the writer, reader, and content. As you contribute your thoughts, the ripple of conversation extends beyond the confines of this book. This act of intimacy, then, resists closure to the conversation, and collectively we orchestrate *Freirean Echoes: Multigenerational Dialogues in Contemporary Times*.

Collective Memory

The core of this book has been stored away for several years, waiting for loving students of Freire to bring it to life. The original group of lectures is a collection of speeches from keynote panelists given at a Critical Pedagogy conference in 2015 hosted by the Paulo Freire Democratic Project, Attallah College of Educational Studies at Chapman University in Orange, California. Over 200 people attended the conference, coming from all parts of the world. Special guest speakers included Dr. Nita Anamaria Freire (Paulo Freire's wife), from Universidade Federal de Mato Grosso, Dr. Antonia Darder, from Loyola Marymount University, Dr. Donaldo Macedo from the University of Massachusetts, and Dr. Peter McLaren and Dr. Tom Wilson, both from Chapman University. A highlight of the event was the rededication of the Paulo Freire Critical Pedagogy Archives housed in the university's Leatherby Libraries. These archives hold Paulo's personal notebook of study, his spectacles, instructional activity cards, and love notes to Nita. The collection also comprises original curriculum developed by Joe Kincheloe, protest posters from all over the world from Peter McLaren, papier-mâché puppets and curriculum developed by Alma Flor Ada, and newspaper clippings and correspondence of Henry Giroux.

While our initial intent was to quickly reproduce the speeches for the public, faculty, and students, resources were not immediately available. Like an aged wine, the original manuscript sat until it distilled a thoughtful design to embrace a dialogical bouquet. The editors, as caring custodians, enacted a pedagogy of collective memory by bringing the past to the present. As we invite you into this conversation, we hope that you escort Freire into future dialogues.

As our project evolved, so did our thinking about the ways we engaged with text. We focused on theorizing "text" as a dialogic space. Often, dialogue is constructed as existing within specific parameters: it can only occur between individuals inhabiting the same physical place, within an exact—and same—physical moment. Thus, dialogue is an action bound by time and space. In other words, we often construe dialogue as authentic only when it lives as "spoken" word, not when it has been "written." As authors, we question this bounded notion of dialogue, and we ask the reader to imagine a possibility where word, world, and action are interwoven through critical engagement with text.

Can Text Be Dialogic?

Frequently, the written word "text" is treated as fixed and inert. It is thought of as an object, differentiated from the changing and iterative processes of living. Dialogue, on the other hand, is dynamic and vibrant. Dialogue can bring about change. When a person commits to undertaking dialogue with another person, both "enter into a co-created reality and transform it. The individual entering the shared space is not afraid to confront, to listen, to see the world unveiled. This person is not afraid to meet people or to enter into dialogue with them" (Freire, 2000, p. 39).

Text can be dialogic. Our goal is to open a conversation that interweaves both text and dialogue as living processes in the service of human engagement and transformative social action. To this end, we have communally created a text. Our hope is that by querying the binary between text and dialogue, people recognize the collective potentiality of dialogic text.

Framing Being and Reading

We begin with the philosophical stance that humans are in a process of "becoming" (Freire, 2001, p. 96). Freire posits this possibility and necessity of change as the driving force of all human action. Becoming, which moves toward more authentic and full existence, is termed "humanization" (Freire, 2000). "Being more," as Freire notes in *Daring to Dream* (2016), is the impetus for human actions that engage the dynamism of history for the sake of revolutionary change (p. 19). Reading, in all of its forms, is one such human process, and it is an act of "becoming."

Arguably, Freire's efforts in literacy, informed as they were by such a vital sense of human existence, led him to be equally and conterminously concerned with the political nature of education. His engagement with reading meant that he examined both the nature of the text/words that were put before him, as well as the nature of the world that those words signified (Freire, 2016). For this reason, Freire (1985) insisted that "the act of reading cannot be explained as merely reading words since every act of reading words implies a previous act of reading the world and a subsequent rereading of the world" (p. 18). Human engagement with the word, therefore, if it is truly authentic to the dynamism of a political being, must include both text and context.

Framing Dialogue

For Freire, one of the foundational modes of coming into critical consciousness, or authentically reading the world, was that of dialogue. He insists: "problem-posing education regards dialogue as indispensable to the act of cognition which unveils reality" (Freire, 2000, p. 71). Dialogue is the active engagement of individuals and perspectives to understand a social phenomenon. As Darder (2017) notes, "dialogue is truly the cornerstone of Freire's pedagogy of love" (p. 90). It is an act of love that is purposeful and political, moving from opinions to theoretical hypothesis and understanding. Dialogue is a political work authentic to human social existence.

Reyes and Torres (2007) remind us that "being human means 'being-in-relation' with other people and with nature as co-creators of culture and participants in its transformation through dialogue" (p. 81). Dialogue, then, is a key step in critical exchanges of knowledge and insight as shared among a community of human beings. It is for the sake of understanding social realities and relations of power. Darder (2017) maintains that

> dialogue is a collaborative phenomenon, with an underlying purpose of building community through participants who focus communally on critical engagements of similar, differing, and contradictory perspectives, in order to understand the world together and forge collective action in the interest of democratic life. (p. 93)

Dialogue is an essential tool for liberation and justice. If, as Paulo Freire (2016) noted in a meeting of students in Brazil, "writing and reading require, in fact, freedom" (p. 49), then so too does the act of engaging in dialogue—an act in which reading and writing ought to be a part.

While dialogue is not *the* most intimate act one can have with a stranger, it can be a very significant experience of connection. It can be rife with naked vulnerabilities and new awakenings. Dialogue is deeply sensual in the probing of mind and heart. It is a loving embrace of each other's ideas with reciprocated empathy and compassion. In dialogue, there can be a passionate interconnectedness wherein two or more people exchange energy and vibrancy that sometimes results in a transformative experience birthing a new dimension of consciousness. Freire and Vittoria (2007) noted: "In the process of dialogue, one ceases to be who she was and allows herself to become another. Knowledge emerges as a reinvention of self" (p. 99).

Darder (2018) describes the conditions of dialogue, stating: "Genuine dialogue can only occur within horizontal relationships within a language of humanization: love, humility, faith, and trust" (p. 122). She further asserts that "dialogue is a co-intentional and co-creative act of human interaction . . . where thoughts will change and new knowledge will be created—knowledge from which new forms of understanding and action will be engendered" (p. 105). Berryman, SooHoo, and Nevin (2013) posit that dialogue is characterized by reciprocity and mutuality. It is a give-and-take. It generates the intention to know, to understand, and to find solidarity in the process of a human exchange. It is a function of being "with" people (Hogg et al., 2020). One must bring one's unfinishedness in an attempt to listen and to learn. According to SooHoo (2013), humility is a vital component of dialogue and relationship building.

What Dialogue Begets

Dialogue—the reciprocal action of sharing our humanity—is a process of mutual knowing and becoming. It is known not in its mechanics, but in identifying what might become as a result of its lived engagement. There is authenticity in true dialogue. In the following sections, we ponder the nature and presence of authentic dialogue. We name some of our musings, and in so doing, we continue to query the ways in which written text engenders a space of "becoming," a space that is dialogic.

Shared Humanity. Dialogue draws us together in action and vision. In a beautiful work, *The Book of Joy* (2016), the Dalai Lama and Archbishop Desmond Tutu explore the virtues and manifestations of joy as captured in a dialogical weekend retreat. They describe their encounter as the bringing together of the familiar heart of strangers. The reader witnesses sweet reciprocity as both men reveal their mutual unfinishedness, contributing life-giving air to each other's ideas. They join each other in conveying a responsibility for the future. Within *The Book of Joy*, the Dalai Lama and Bishop Tutu spend two days interacting in loving dialogue, in sensing selves, feeling each other's face, laughing at each other's jokes, and respecting each other's difference. Their dialogue shares a common vision for humanity.

A Praxis of Togetherness. Dialogue is a process of "bestowing recognition rather than invisibility on others" (Greene, 2009, p. 117). It is *touching* the consciousness of those we meet. When we are in dialogue, it is possible to explore untapped possibilities. We can more clearly see who we are when in communion with another. Dialogue, Greene concludes, allows us to receive a renewed consciousness of worth and possibility.

In Toni Morrison's famous book *Beloved* (1987), there is a passage of a character describing his friend: "She is a friend of mine. She gather me, man. The pieces I am, she gathers them and give them back to me all in the right order. It's good, you know, when you got a woman who is a friend of your mind" (pp. 272–273). From a dialogically enriched vantage point, one can reinvent one's self within a praxis of togetherness (SooHoo et al., 2019).

Conditions for Democracy. Spaces of democracy evidence the presence of dialogue. True democracy does not allow for a dichotomy between our political goals and the means by which we seek to attain them. Critical scholar Timothy Bolin (2017) notes that "where the goal is democracy, a democratic process *is* essential, because the goal of democracy is fundamental to the process of democracy" (p. 761). In this sense, democracy is always in the making. Koczanowicz (2015) notes that democracy includes "essentially a struggle for the right to speak in the name of 'the people'" (p. 92). We might, in fact, expand this concept to say that democracy is a struggle to speak *as a people*. Democracy, therefore, requires dialogue.

As members of a democratic community, it is our civic responsibility to be well informed; to listen to others to broaden our perspectives. This type of civic engagement is made possible through dialogue. Koczanowicz (2015) notes:

> Dialogue is, thus, at the same time an outcome and a premise of understanding, as for an act of understanding to take place, an interaction between the word of the speaker and the conceptual horizon of the listener is necessary, and the outcome of such interaction is a significant change in the conceptual systems of both the speaker and the listener. (p. 56)

Democracy is always unfinished, ongoing, multi-ethnic, multi-generational. It is engendered through dialogic processes that establish new solidarity and build communities of critical understanding.

Problem Posing. Kincheloe maintains that teachers need to engage with students in constant dialogue that works to question existing knowledge and problematizes the traditional power relations that have served to marginalize specific groups and individuals (Kincheloe & McLaren, 1994). His problem-posing stance harnesses our collaborative human curiosity and leads us to ask questions such as: How can we better address the problem in our every-day lives in ethically socially responsible ways? What systems underlie the current issue facing us? Which missing voices speak to these issues?

As we interact in dialogue and with such questions, we come to a shared mutuality. We come together in a space of ideas that did not exist prior to our collaborative interaction. This shared locale is a liminal space (McLaren, 1988; Bhabha, 1994; Soja, 1996). It is a space of production and can be a place for recapturing history and projecting future possibilities as we name the world. This liminal space is a site for untested feasibility and of potential critical consciousness.

Possibility Posing. In dialogue, venues of "imaginative social possibilities" (Greene, 2009, p. 9) can take shape and allow us to re-shape our limited situations, the existential circumstances that impede our ability to be fully human (Jaspers & Grabau, 1971; Freire, 1970; Petruzzi, 1998). Darder (2018) states that "limit situations are perceived as the frontier between being and being more human" (p. 135). "Human possibilities," she notes, "lie just beyond the[se] limit-situations, which often remain obscured" (p. 135). Not only do we come to grasp these limit-situations, but dialogue enables us to do more, to imagine a world as yet unknown. Dialogue allows us to imagine the possible. As Greene (2009) reminds us, "imagination breathes life into experience" (p. 22) and provides new pathways when "our lives narrow and our pathways become cul-de-sacs" (p. 17). Imagination defies fatalism and offers hope to dream a new utopia. As we ground these utopias in real-life opportunities, we engage in a form of freedom that presents alternative possibilities for our becoming. Possibility thinking "lessens the social paralysis that we see around us and restores the sense that something can be done in the name of what is decent and humane" (p. 35).

Action. Dialogue can take many shapes. Greene (2009) proposes various forms to teachers:

> . . . dialogue among the young who come from different cultures and different modes of life, dialogue among people who have come together to solve problems that seem worth solving to all of them, dialogue among people undertaking shared tasks, protesting injustices, avoiding or overcoming dependences or illnesses. (p. 5)

Thus, dialogue can be the catalyst for action as well as the medium of sense-making of the action we are already engaged in. It provides communal feedback, opportunities to adjust worldviews, and a way to harness energy from the collective when we ask, "What can we do together that we cannot do alone?"

Theory Building. Action is the ground/soil/seeds from which our theories develop. Praxis, therefore, is the reciprocal dialogue between action and reflection. We understand that theories do not emerge in isolation and that the extension of theory into praxis requires ongoing learning. Our theories, then, develop in sync with lived realities that are continually interrogated, deepened, and sharpened (Monzó, 2019). Shor (1987) maintains that critical literacy and dialogical learning occurs when the concrete world intersects with the academic world. Further, he pushes us to consider that education must promote both emancipatory change and the cultivation of the intellect. These goals should never be in conflict; they should be synergistic. Dialogue allows us to learn alongside others as we continue in the work of theory building.

Social Transformation. We recall Freire's (2000) statement: "There is no true word that is not at the same time a praxis. Thus, to speak a true word is to transform the world" (p. 75). As we come together in lively interchange concerning social relations and contexts, there ought to be movement of a dialogical community from theory into action. Freire (2001) writes: "Insofar as I am a conscious presence in the world, I cannot hope to escape my ethical responsibility for my action in the world" (p. 26). Through dialogue, our social responsibility to transform our world is given collective and meaningful contextual direction.

Examples of Dialogic Spaces

Freire warns that "action is human only when it is not merely an occupation but also a preoccupation, that is, when it is not dichotomized from reflection" (2000, p. 38). Just as humans are ever becoming in their consciousness and relationships in the world, so too does the cycle of dialogue and praxis find itself intertwined in a never-ending process of unfolding. Like human action, dialogue in its many forms is imperfect and ought to lead to reflection. When we have struggled together for change, we must ask how we have impacted the world and what limits remain and/or are created by our work (Freire, 2016).

Freire's framework insists that reflection is the essential connection between theory and action. Reflection is, in some sense, the exercising of the imagination, seeing not only the limits of our work, but also the "untested feasibility" of the future (Freire, 2016). Reflecting on text and/as/with/through dialogue, we echo the question of Maxine Greene (2009): "how can we communicate the importance of opening spaces in the imagination where persons can reach beyond where they are" (p. 86). We can do this only through an invitation to dialogue, praxis, and reflection.

Text can be a space of becoming with the reader, a place of dialogue, a moment in the cycle of praxis. These processes take many names and forms, as Suzanne SooHoo notes (personal communication, 7/11/17): "No matter what you want to call it, the work includes an examination of practice and policy, uses literature and dialogue for the purpose of the common good, with the specific intention of creating spaces for marginalized and alienated groups." In other words, text can occupy a space where iterative and just processes are central in the transformation of the world.

We do not, however, propose that all text and/or encounters-with-text are dialogic. Just as we are able to act in ways that are anti-communal and oppressive, so too are we able to read and write in ways that are not open to possibility-positioned exchanges. The nature of dialogue requires the cooperative presence and openness of more than one party. As such, the dialogic possibility of text requires that both the reader and the text are positioned as open.

In reading text, context is an important consideration. It is possible to read only to memorize or be entertained. While not negative, these ways of reading are not dialogic processes. One can read and interpret texts without drawing connections to self, or to the real world. A text in this mechanical context cannot be a space of dialogue. But there are ways to open up such dialogic possibilities. We see this in book clubs and in reading circles where participants engage in a shared experience through text and community. Fruitful and authentic dialogue is possible here because the text becomes a space from which realities such as collective learning, problem posing, and theory building can take place. Texts themselves are not dialogue, but in the context of open and reflective reading, texts can become literary locations and liminal spaces, in which dialogue is shaped.

The form a text takes can work to open it into a dialogic space or keep it confined. It is not the content of text that makes it dialogic. Rather, it is the reading of text that evokes life and dialogue. In this way, text may take a form that mirrors face-to-face interchanges. A few key elements of dialogic form might include: (a) the presence of multiple voices or perspectives in the text; (b) the presentation of unresolved social problems without an authoritative attempt to answer them; (c) using a genre of text that helps the reader to perceive the content in new ways; and (d) the inclusion of questions directed at the reader.

One historical example of text that has become a dialogic space is the Torah when accompanied by Midrash. Midrash is text on the margins surrounding the text of the Torah that offers new understandings or interpretations. Here, the sacred text is surrounded by interpretive notes authored by religious scholars over many centuries. Levinson (2004) notes: "This simultaneity of two narratives is at the heart of dialogic reading. The reader not only interprets the midrashic narrative against the background of the biblical story, but also reinterprets the biblical story against the background of the midrash" (p. 505). This literary form invites one to engage with the Torah as well as the reflections of these ancient scholars, opening a space for rich exchange. Thus, text can be a dialogic space when it intends and requires the interchange and engagement of the reader(s).

We are not coming into this inquiry without reflection and praxis. It has been our tradition as authors to make the recent books we have worked on align with Freirean thought in the writing process, literary form, and content. *Let's Chat: Cultivating Community University Dialogue* (2019) was constructed through co-crafting every word and idea as a community of authors. We hoped the book would engage our readers in dialogue as well. To facilitate this, each chapter ended with questions posed as "cafecitos" (coffee chats) in which readers can enter the conversation with the text and arrive at new possibilities in their lives. In *Pedagogies of With-ness: Students, Teachers, Voice and Agency* (2021), authors from New Zealand and the United States wrote about their understanding and experience of voice and agency in education. In drawing these voices together around a central reality, the text became a space where these works informed each other. By using a larger mediating metaphor of art galleries, the text invited the reader to engage with author voices as well as their own form of justice-informed action in the world.

*Freirean Echoes: Multigenerational Dialogues in Contemporary Time*s employs the concept of *echo* to conceptualize the ways in which scholars, activists, teachers, and others have continued the work of Paulo Freire. We have chosen a sonar metaphor to address our original query, "Can text be dialogic?" Indeed, we believe that it can be, and we see this in acts of amplification and reverberation.

As we define it, amplification is the magnification of a sound or idea. It increases volume, enlarging or adding detail to an original resonance. When a chapter author amplifies a message, she/he is saying, "I hear you. This is what I understand you to be saying. This is what it means to me. This is how it relates to my life, my vision. As I stand in your shoes, this is what I hear." Authors who amplify an original idea facilitate a message in ways that are unobstructed and take care to make more perceptible the finer elements of the messages they reflect upon. Like the air that acts as the medium through which sound waves move, these authors serve to move the message forward so that others may hear it. They ensure that others may have access to the richness of these ideas. Thus amplification is one-directional. It is the original message shared out.

For us, reverberation is resonance, sound with continuing impact. A reverberant sound is the response and collective reality of all sounds interacting in an environment. It includes a secondary effect. It is a repercussion. A sound wave becomes reverberant when it strikes a *thing* and takes a new direction and tonal quality because of this encounter. A visual of the collective dimension of reverberation would show sonar scans that ping back a pattern of dots on new terrain. In this book, chapter authors respond to the original ping/idea/speaker, informed by new contexts and experiences, giving the original messages new trajectories. This echoing effect, which creates new ideological pathways, is the dialogical genesis of new conceptual territory for critical pedagogy.

Our Book Structure

The scholars in *Freirean Echoes: Multigenerational Dialogues in Contemporary Times* are philosophical kin to the Paulo Freire Democratic Project. As they turn to one another within the book, their essays evoke Paulo's spirit and his enduring philosophy on the centrality of dialogue. However, it was not until we began to construct the book that we asked about the ability of text to be a space of dialogue. This was more than a question of accessibility of text; it was also about *encounterability* through text. Within the pages of this book, could we create a space in which authors and readers interact in and through text via dialogue? Together, could the ideas be amplified and reverberated in new ways and with new meanings?

We have purposely been attuned to the form our writing takes in constructing this text, shifting the form-content relationship by positioning form *as* content. Each chapter opens with a speech by an established scholar and is followed by two written responses (one by a scholar and the other by a practitioner). These responses intentionally engage the ideas of the opening speech. Ultimately, the authors hand the talking stick to you, the readers, inviting another ring of amplifications and reverberations. We encourage you through section questions and activities to engage with the reading in thought and action, bringing the dialogue forward into your worlds.

Section One of the book centers on Nita Freire's keynote, "The Presence of Paulo Freire at Chapman University" as she ponders Paulo's concept of untested-feasibility. Anaida Colón-Muñiz and Edgar Orejel reverberate Nita's thoughts by interpreting hope and possibility within their own contexts.

In Section Two, we read the work of Tom Wilson on his development and use of a pedagogical method that engages students in dialogical critical thinking. Suzanne SooHoo amplifies this work by showing Wilson's elegant alignment of critical thinking with the moral development of critical consciousness. Greg Warren delineates the scholarly lineage of Wilson's work and reverberates a new dimension and considers the future possibilities of this pedagogy.

In Section Three, we encounter Peter McLaren's early articulation of his spiritual re-awakening and its impact on the historical project of liberatory education. Petar Jandrić responds in a written dialogue with McLaren elaborating on the need to develop critical pedagogy toward human-technology relationships and critical posthumanism. Charlotte Achieng-Evensen and Kevin Stockbridge engage with McLaren's musings and the significance of those musings on *positionality*, *epistemology*, and *pedagogy* in public education.

In Section Four, Antonia Darder reflects upon the ongoing nature of struggle as it pertains to democratization and economic justice. Darder makes explicit the idea of unrelenting evolution—social justice action requires continual maintenance. Lilia Monzó amplifies and undergirds Antonia's work by elucidating Marx's concept of absolute negativity as constitutive of liberation. Kimberley White-Smith integrates family wisdom and the context of Black Lives Matter in her deliberation of justice.

In Section Five, Donaldo Macedo brings to the forefront the "academification of oppression." He cautions against and counters the utility of social justice for the purposes of cultivating an academic pedigree. Cathery Yeh, while embracing her position as junior scholar, interrogates the processes she must undergo as a faculty member. Christian Bracho muses on Macedo's concept of coherence and its implications for his practice as a teacher educator.

In the Afterword of *Freirean Echoes*, the book draws to a close by presenting to the readers the relevance of the work in our current social context of the Covid pandemic and political unrest.

Concluding Thoughts

As we began this work, we posited that text, when constructed thoughtfully and intentionally, can cultivate generative spaces of rich interchange and collective imagining. When positioned as unfinished, text as a space for engaged dialogue authentically reflects human existence and interconnectedness. As editors, we see text as especially dialogic when received through the lens of possible social change. As Freirean practice, text is an imaginary space for human dialogue, a generative location for social justice praxis, and a historical dreamscape for reflection.

The significance of this work is that it is collective. It stands in opposition to creating unilateral answers for educational and social problems. It prioritizes a process in which the reader and author inhabit a shared space of human becoming. Moving from a prescriptive and deterministic idea of text, this book invites consideration of the many possibilities for the written word to become a lived, authentic moment of dialogue. That is, there can be no single text or idea which answers all human concerns. Rather, dialogic textual interaction is most fertile when multiple voices co-write, co-read, co-live, and co-make the world.

References

Berryman, M., SooHoo, S., & Nevin, A. (2013). *Culturally responsive methodologies*. Emerald.

Bhabha, H.K. (1994). *The location of culture*. Routledge.

Bolin, T.D. (2017). Struggling for democracy: Paulo Freire and transforming society through education. *Policy Futures in Education*, 15(6), 744–766. https://doi.org/10.1177/1478210317721311

Dalai Lama, Tutu, D., & Abrams, D.C. (2016). *The book of joy: Lasting happiness in a changing world*. Penguin Random House.

Darder, A. (2017). *Reinventing Paulo Freire: A pedagogy of love*. Routledge.

Darder, A. (2018). *The student guide to Freire's pedagogy of the oppressed*. Bloomsbury.

Freire, A., & Vittoria, P. (2007). Dialogue on Paulo Freire. *Interamerican Journal of Education for Democracy*, 1(1), 97–117.
Freire, P. (1970). The adult literacy process as cultural action for freedom. *Harvard Educational Review*, 40(2), 205–225.
Freire, P. (1985). Reading the word and reading the world: An interview with Paulo Freire. *Language Arts*, 62(1), 15–21.
Freire, P. (1998). *Pedagogy of freedom: Ethics, democracy, and civic courage.* Rowman & Littlefield.
Freire, P. (2000). *Pedagogy of the oppressed.* Continuum.
Freire, P. (2001). *Pedagogy of freedom: Ethics, democracy, and civic courage.* Continuum.
Freire, P. (2016). *Daring to dream: Toward a pedagogy of the unfinished.* Routledge.
Greene, M. (2009). In search of a critical pedagogy. In A. Darder, M.P. Baltodano, & R.D. Torres (Eds.), *The critical pedagogy reader* (2nd ed.), pp. 84–96. Routledge.
Hogg, L., Stockbridge, K., Achieng-Evensen, C., & SooHoo, S. (2020). *Pedagogies of with-ness: Students, teachers, voice, and agency.* Myers Education Press.
Jaspers, K., & Grabau, R. (1971). *Philosophy of existence.* University of Pennsylvania Press. www.jstor.org/stable/j.ctt3fhpdv
Kincheloe, J., & McLaren, P. (1994). Rethinking critical theory and qualitative research. In N. Denzin & Y. Lincoln (Eds.), *Handbook of qualitative research*, (pp. 138–157). Sage.
Koczanowicz, L. (2015). *Politics of dialogue: Non-consensual democracy and critical community.* Edinburgh University Press.
Levinson, J. (2004). Dialogical reading in the rabbinical narrative. *Poetics Today*, 25(3), 497–528.
McLaren, P. (1988). The liminal servant and the ritual roots of critical pedagogy. *Language Arts*, 65(2), 164–179.
Monzó, L.D. (2019). *A revolutionary subject: Pedagogy of women of color and indigeneity.* Peter Lang.
Morrison, T. (1987). *Beloved.* Random House.
Petruzzi, A. (1998). Between conventions and critical thinking: The concept of "limit-situations" in critical literacy and pedagogy. *JAC*, 18(2), 309–332. www.jstor.org/stable/20866187
Reyes, L.V., & Torres, M.N. (2007). Decolonizing family literacy in a culture circle: Reinventing the family educator's role. *Journal of Early Childhood Literacy*, 7(1), 73–94.
Shor, I., & Freire, P. (1987). *A pedagogy for liberation: Dialogues on transforming education.* Bergin & Garvey.
Soja, E.W. (1996). *Thirdspace: Journeys to Los Angeles and other real-and-imagined places.* Blackwell.
SooHoo, S. (2013). Humility within culturally responsive methodologies. In M. Berryman, S. SooHoo, & A. Nevin (Eds.), *Culturally responsive methodologies*, (pp. 199–220). Emerald.
SooHoo, S., Huerta, P., Huerta-Meza, P.P., Bolin, T., & Stockbridge, K. (2019). *Let's chat: Cultivating community university dialogue.* Myers Education Press.

Section One

CHAPTER ONE

The Presence of Paulo Freire at Chapman University

Ana Maria Araújo Freire

My return to Chapman University is, by itself, a fact that gives me great joy as I remember the tributes that Paulo Freire, my husband, received in 1998—the title of Doctor Honoris Causa and the inauguration of his sculpture at the Chapman campus.

The affection that I received from the President James L. Doti, from Mrs. Paula Hassinger—a generous collaborator of this university in the genuine interest of perpetuating the name of her husband—as well as the love from faculty and students were unforgettable. Also, I remember the undeniable support I received from Tom Wilson and Peter Park, faithful friends of Paulo and mine, who joined me in those moments of joy and gladness, while at the same time mourned with me the enormous pain I carried from the still recent loss of Paulo.

I want to greet all present at this ceremony through the following valued people whom I met sixteen years ago: President Doti; Don Cardinal, Dean of the College of Educational Studies; Daniele Struppa, the Chancellor who funded the symposium; and Charlene Baldwin, Dean of the Libraries. Upon my return, it is also my pleasure to see once again old friends such as Tom Wilson and Peter Park, who are examples of honesty and loyalty, men of caliber and ethics in their personal, intellectual, and professional lives, and Suzanne SooHoo—Suzi, as we call her. It is also a huge thrill for me to see Peter McLaren and Donaldo Macedo, who through discussions and dialogue became old friends in work and friendship, partners of ideological and theoretical ideas of Paulo. They, along with Henry Giroux, formulated **critical pedagogy** as we know of it today.

Now, I have not only come to receive homage for my husband Paulo Freire; I have also come to make an official donation on behalf of Paulo and myself to Chapman University. As you may know, these documents were my property and in my possession until 2008, when I originally donated them to McGill University, Canada. More specifically, I donated them to the now extinct "Paulo and Nita Freire International Project for Critical Pedagogy." As the official holder of those objects and by virtue of my Letter of Donation signed in 2014 by Chapman and myself, these documents now belong to this university.

The event today represents for me a very special moment. It gives me peace to know that this material, in accordance with current international law, belongs to a collection that values the man and the educator that was Paulo Freire.

The letters, files, and journal with personal notes about famous Brazilian and foreign authors, including the very glasses Paulo wore to write these, are part of this collection. I consider **all handwritten** notes as emblematic pieces of his being in the world. These notes represent his body and his mind, and his fruitful presence in the world. After many aimless comings and goings to different parts of Canada and the United States, without care, abandoned, being touched by anyone as they pleased, being photographed by any hands and without appreciation of this material heritage of my husband, these belongings have finally found their utopian residence, where, I hope, it will never depart. It is my expectation that here at Chapman University this collection will remain, so that students and teachers can seriously use it in their scientific or philosophical research. Moreover, it is my wish that researchers become enchanted with the beauty with which Paulo engraved in his writings the brilliant and poetic words of scientific and educational character—all of them written with love and with ethical seriousness. This is why I cannot imagine the possession of this material by particular individuals, no matter how well-intentioned they are.

I want. at this solemn moment, to enrich my donation with a Doctor Honoris Causa degree awarded to Paulo by the Oldenburg University, Germany, which I received personally on July 7, 1997, just days after his death. I must clarify that it is the practice of this university to issue two documents, which they consider originals. Thus, one of them will stay in Brazil, the beloved homeland of Paulo, and mine, forever. The other I offer to enlarge the collection I donated to Chapman University in confidence that this will bring delight among members of this academic community.

It is important to reiterate that except for a few loose papers—mostly letters sent by Paulo himself during his lifetime—all material that now belongs to this university is and will forever be the only one legitimately and legally existent outside of Brazil. All documents of Paulo, including the Documentary Collection, are considered "Public Interest and National Social Heritage," and they are prohibited to leave the Brazilian territory by Decree of May 9, 2012, signed by President Dilma Rousseff.

I do not doubt the honesty of those at Chapman who fought to retain this collection here at the university. It is still a small collection, but of great value for the history of progressive ideas and for those who truly want to study the thought of Paulo Freire. My request to the entire community of Chapman University is this: Keep these documents with care and affection, as rarity, as a relic indeed, which was produced by the intelligence and sensitivity of the "educator of critical consciousness," the Patron of Brazilian Education.[1]

At this point, I dare to propose to Chapman University to become a radiating center in the United States to promote the thought and research about my husband Paulo Freire, respecting him as the greatest educator of the twentieth century, of the entire world. I hope that the readings and research that will take place here go beyond his best-known book, *Pedagogy of the Oppressed*, because Paulo cannot be reduced or minimized as the author of only one book. Throughout his life, he continued to write with wisdom, experience, and intellectual generosity until the last moments of his life. Books such as *Pedagogy of Freedom* (Pedagogia da Autonomia) and *Pedagogy of Indignation* (Pedagogia da Indignação)—one which I organized and gave name to—should be mandatory to anyone who truly wants to know the educator for liberation. These books are both fruits of Paulo's intellectual and personal political maturity and emotional acuity, and they are among several other books of his own, already translated into English. In addition, the center that I dream of for this university should have copies of his books in at least the Portuguese, Spanish, and French languages, in addition to the English language.

At this point, I would like to say a few words about how Paulo conceived the concept of **untested-feasibility**, motivated by this **untested-feasibility**: the desire of Chapman University to have the collection of my husband within its walls. The scholars at the university knew the importance of having the collection here, and because of this, what was an **untested-feasibility** has now been made concrete and has become a **testing action**—consolidated.

The **untested-feasibility** is not a mere combination of letters or an idiomatic expression lacking meaning. It is a more rigorous word in a Freirean perspective. It is a word-action and therefore implies praxis. It is a word epistemologically constructed to express—with enormous emotional, cognitive, political, ethical, and ontological charge—the projects and actions of human possibilities. It is a word that brings in itself the germ of possible transformations geared toward a more humane and ethical future. It carries within itself the beliefs, values, dreams, desires, aspirations, fears, anxieties, the yearning and ability to learn, and the fragility and greatness of human beings. A word that conveys a sound restlessness and beauty rooted within the human condition. In this word, duty and taste are intrinsic, as Paulo used to say, changing us dialectically while changing the world and being changed by the world. This word brings in its own essence what we feel, desire, fight, and dream. Moreover, it brings to light what bothers us, what makes us dissatisfied and sad at the weaknesses of human beings driven by real ingenuity or by the deformation of anti-ethicity.

The **untested-feasibility** contains in itself the comprehension of time and space, a denunciation and an announcement. It is in this time and space in which we, "patiently impatient," foster the epistemological curiosity that should lead to philosophical and scientific knowledge. It leads to the implementation of ontological and historical hope through transformative creativity of human dreams. Science and philosophy that do not promote these feasible dreams, and the incarnation of the **untested-feasibility** materialized in the **testing action,** do not deserve our respect and consideration. It is not science; it is scientism. It is not philosophy; it is philosophism.

The **untested-feasibility** concept has created a new epistemology from a hopeful new reading of the world. It drives us to create a new man and a new woman for a new, less ugly, more democratic, more just society, which is what Paulo has long emphasized in his teachings. As mentioned earlier, when the problem is already a **background-awareness**, the concept of "**untested-feasibility**" provides the necessary unity of this lucidity, joy, and transparency of the dream, in which an ontologically human process is presented as possible. In addition, as a **background-awareness**, the concept shows the past of injustice, torment, and suffering that afflicted us to the point that we realized prominently that it is a problem awaiting a solution. Finally, the concept points out the welcoming future quietly unsettling, the peace of conscience for the rescue of ethicity, and the feeling of making sure that everything goes, needs, and must continue through an uninterrupted process of changes in order to concretize the ever-changing **Being More** of everyone and all of us.

The **untested-feasibility** tells us clearly that there is no definitive, ready, or finished kingdom; nor the nirvana of certainty or perfect stillness. Reaching out to the **untested-feasibility** which we dream of and strive for, means not only dreaming about what would be possible but dreaming about the **possible dream,** of the achieved utopia, which brings forth other **untested-feasibility**, as many as can fit in our feelings and our reason dictated by our most authentically human needs. These dreams, whilest word-praxis, are connected radically and essentially to what is most ontologically human in us: the hope that exists in the movements of perfecting our social-historical construction and ourselves for Peace and Justice. The more we can dream and concretize the **untested-feasibility,** the more it will unfold and proliferate within our praxis, within our political desires, within the affirmative destiny of our most authentic humanity, and within our ingenious ability to overcome and project ourselves onto a fertile and infinite world of possibilities.

Furthermore, Paulo understood the **untested-feasibility** as a strategy, meaning the possibility of taking concrete actions regarding our longings, needs, desires, and dreams, socially intended, engaged, and realized at every moment by the **background-awareness** actions, as we approach what actions are historically possible in a given time. Among these, **democracy** and the realization of **Being More** have primacy because they are, in fact, the strategies to be achieved, and they correspond to the fulfillment of the ontological vocation of all human beings.

The richness of the concept of **untested-feasibility** developed by Paulo in *Pedagogy of the Oppressed*, and further advanced in *Pedagogy of Hope*, is actually of great importance and depth. It "soaks" (to use an expression dear to him) all of his work, because it translates his coherent way of reading the world. Called so by him intentionally, not to hold onto its linguistic beauty, but for its semantic richness, it opens up to a genuinely human world—that is, the world of ethics and liberation. In his critical analysis, the **untested-feasibility** indicates multiple wishes, desires, needs, wants, reason, creation, and, above all, a spirit of justice.

The qualities/feelings that exist within us were guided by ethical seriousness and were collectively engendered, so that when realized step by step through tactical action, they will certainly reach the ultimate ending of the **untested-feasibility**. Utopia, the most radical of these, which (paradoxically), in order to maintain its own characteristic—the field of **possible dream**, which is nourished by our no less important human inconclusiveness—is not an end, but a definite term of arrival. Therefore, it is up to Utopia to overcome what has been accomplished, which will be transitory in the ethical path to fulfill the ontological vocation of every human being **to be more.** Further, the democracy in its ethnic, sexual, racial, religious, and social dimensions—since there cannot be one without the other—requires remaking it dialectically in the search for improvement.

Paulo understood human subjectivity in a unique way. He showed us how not to limit ourselves to the subject-object dialectic in order to act, transform, or know, while adjusting ourselves to any necessary conditions of the given world. That is, Paulo understood this relationship to radicalize our subjectivities in such a way that we, as subjects that relate to each other mediated by the objective world, could build not only knowledge, but also conditions and relations of knowledge of historical and axiological appeal to change the human future. Paulo understood that we are not mere spectators of history who are randomly passing without making any interference. Like many other thinkers, he understood that we are not a reflection of reality or that we constitute reality from the simple idea of making it. Thus, he recognized that reality is constructed by the relationships between our consciousness and daily life consisting of observing, creating, doing, remaking, sensing, understanding, feeling, perceiving, grasping, and systematizing what the natural and cultural world offers or imposes upon us. From this understanding of what constitutes reality, the **possible dreams** are ultimately cultural products that our subjectivities could build. They are also the agents and products that constitute and mobilize re-creation, thus potentially contributing to the politico-social transformation. If any of us think about changing the world alone, through a solitary relationship between ourselves and the world already given, we would know in a short time that this is not a **possible dream**; it is a schizophrenic daydream without possibilities. It is not an **untested-feasibility.**

The **untested-feasibility**, besides being a collective dream, should always be at the service of the community, for it has no purpose in itself. Therefore, it is fundamentally democratic in the service of what is most human in us: the fulfillment of our ontological vocation **to be more** in permanent process of liberation. The concept of **untested-feasibility,** in Paulo's understanding of education and society, is intentionally developed to make us feel indignation, righteous anger, and repudiation. It calls us to mobilize ourselves in denial of these feelings, compelling us to take actions. It also gives us a more exact dimension of our political, ethical, and aesthetic abilities, and our need for justice and peace. Moreover, it conveys Paulo's intentionality to make us reflect the possibility of human vocation **to be more,** and to act guided by ethics and political will toward **possible dreams.**

We need to believe in our potential to dream as Paulo did. In his theory of knowledge, he emphasized two dimensions, which dialectically complement each other: the liberating and dialogic aspects of education and the need for a more just and humane society, a utopia to be achieved. When his theory was conceived and proclaimed, it constituted an **untested-feasibility** in itself, and many did not believe in its consistency and necessity. Many considered him a dreamer of ineffective dreams. Today, if we still have not achieved the dream in its fullness, we have reached the realization that we can fight for this dream as a **possible dream,** even when facing threats of all sorts that hit us in times of violence generated mainly by neoliberalism and the globalization of the economy. Unfortunately, the anti-ethicity that strikes the world today makes it uglier and more perverse.

If the work of Paulo is absolutely impregnated and full of **untested-feasibilities,** it is due not only to his known coherent posture between **to be** and **to think,** but also to his ability to dream, predicting a future that we can build. His work and his praxis, and even his personal view of the world—his peopleness—reveal him as an **untestedly-feasibility** being: an embodied being; a thinking being; a person who acts in the world with love. Paulo has created an understanding of education, nurtured by ethical and political content, which contributed to the history of world progressive pedagogical ideas.

I would like to say that Paulo grasped by intuition, sensitivity, and reason the **limit situations** of our Brazilian society. This was made possible by his analysis of how we organized ourselves economically and socially and by his reading about the secular conditions of oppression, supported by, among others, an elitist and authoritarian education, impaired and retrograde, theoretically speaking, and thus "banking" for that matter. For all these reasons, Paulo constitutes himself in fact, an **untested-feasibility**. It was Paulo, and not another, who told us all what he said, who understood with absolute, unprecedented clarity the relationship between education, ethics, and politics. He raised his voice and denounced, and executed his claims through his **limit-situations**—among which, I emphasize, his own theoretical creation and, in it, the understanding of **untested-feasibility**—precisely because he knew how to capture, with blatant obviousness, what the world was saying and crying out while we were not listening. Because he had humility and the wisdom to make himself aware within his own historical limitations, he could propose to us to overcome the narrow limits imposed by denying the ontological human vocation to **Be More**, through the hope that is built into **untested-feasibility**—thus, announcing through **untested-feasibility**, embedded in it, the hopeful foretaste of the viable. In this sense, to denounce in the presence of what is rejected, dehumanizing, unethical, which the **untested-feasibility** itself reveals, is indeed a utopian dream, loaded with generosity, humanity, and hope in the future.

Certainly, there are others who do not embody **untested-feasibilities** because they do not have the ability to grasp reality; or because they do not have sensitivity for this matter; or even because of the **peopleness** problems of us all, which means the problems affecting us all. These problems refer especially to education, to the disenfranchised, and to the poor, which are issues of transcendental dimension and religions, and not of the educators. They are problems of serious or unscrupulous politicians, not problems of those with a citizenship mindset. They are problems of those who care only about themselves and their peers, those who consider the problems of the people—the needy and hungry—as crimes. Especially when the victims protest, they think the problems need to be solved by the police, and not to be settled by themselves, who think about **"the national sovereignty."** For them, it does not matter what people know or do not know, nor what they want or need, or what they teach us through common sense. Antagonistically, Paulo did philosophy from the problems of everyday life, embodying them with compassion and reason in an **untested-feasibility** of humanism and justice. Precisely because he felt, seized, listened, analyzed, and systematized all that was there to be seen and thought, in its surroundings, in the obviousness of everyday life, he was able to see what nobody had seen. Paulo took the problems and gave them a philosophical-sociological and ontological forum. He converted these problems into fundamental questions of *human existence*, which impel us, therefore, to continue clarifying and resolving all that remains unsolved. And it is for us a **background-awareness**, as it was for Paulo, years ago, in his intelligent and sensitive consciousness.

By saying that Paulo was an **untested-feasible** being as a result of his historical and personal circumstances, I am saying, in other words, he was a prophet. As a prophet who can "foresee" the problems and anticipate the perception thereof, he presented us a path to solve them. Certainly, he did not present us solutions. Otherwise, he would not have been the prophet of hope, but the creator of the already pre-determined reality, the owner of the humans and the world, which by controlling the actions and future instances would have taken away from us the possibility of being the builders of our History. He would not have been the man he was, dialogical and liberating, because he would not have had the exceptional ability to love his life so passionately. Moreover, he would not have had the ability to be generous and tolerant, to believe in other human beings, and to believe that there are difficult things for which we must seek strength in **historical possibilities** precisely because, as humans, we are limited by our inconclusiveness. In this way, Paulo made us believe that things are the way they are "not because they were always like that," or "because God wants them this way," or "because changing the social and political order (called natural) of things is impossible." Paulo showed us the way: the **possible dream** of a better future, providing that today we strive for the **untested-feasibilities**, the utopias, of our current time.

These are Paulo's words in his book, which I organized and named *Pedagogy of Indignation:*

> Thinking of tomorrow is thus engaging in prophecy, except that the prophet in this case is not an old man with a long and gray beard, with lively open eyes and stave in hand, hardly concerned about his attire, preaching incensed words. On the contrary, the prophets here are those who are founded in what they live, in what they see, hear, apprehend, in what they understand, who are rooted in their epistemological curiosity exercise, alert to signs they seek to comprehend, supported in their reading of the world and of words new and old, which is the base of how and how much they expose themselves, thus becoming more and more a presence in the world at a par with their

> time. They speak almost predicting, in fact as if intuiting what may occur in this or that dimension of their social-historical experience. (2004, p. 104)

Paulo made prophecy without staff and without hallucinations. He made true prophecies, predictions of what he wanted to see done because he was sure that they corresponded to human dreams in general, that is, from the concrete dreams of those who had lived and communed with him. He gave a name, a word, for this act of faith and **possible dream** as a powerful result generated by the possibility that we, men and women, have an intentional and collective pursuit to make ourselves more authentically human—building a more just, joyful, and fraternal society: the **Freirean untested-feasibility**.

In conclusion, I say that it is here in this space—a space which is open to scientific and pedagogical debate, a space that is eminently political, and a space destined to attest what we know or do not know; what we can learn or what we already know by analyzing our pedagogical practices and contributions to the academic discussions—that we ultimately discover a time and space where we, by **enabling unprecedentedly** the fulfillment of the democratic dreams, necessarily and "Freireanly," educate people to **Be More.**

PAULO FREIRE LIVES AT CHAPMAN UNIVERSITY.
HE LIVES WITHIN THE HEARTS OF MEN AND WOMEN
WHO LOVE LIFE!

References

Freire, P. (1970). *Pedagogy of the oppressed.* Continuum.

Freire, P. (1992). *Pedagogy of hope: Reliving pedagogy of the oppressed.* Continuum.

Freire, P. (2001). *Pedagogy of freedom: Ethics, democracy, and civic courage.* Rowman & Littlefield.

Freire, P. (2004). *Pedagogy of indignation.* Paradigm.

Endnote

[1] Lei no. 12.612, de 13 de abril de 2012, assinada pela Presidenta Dilma Rousseff.

CHAPTER TWO

Untested Feasibility:
My Reflection on Paulo and Nita Freire's Hope for Utopia

ANAIDA COLÓN-MUÑIZ

IN THIS TIME OF untested feasibility, I reflect upon the words of the great educational philosopher Paulo Freire and his life partner and widow, Ana Maria Araújo "Nita" Freire. Nita visited Chapman University a number of years ago during a Critical Pedagogy symposium hosted by the Paulo Freire Democratic Project (PFDP). At that time, we held the Rededication of the Paulo Freire Archives, at which Nita made significant donations to the archives for the Special Collections of Leatherby Libraries. During that visit, she also received a Distinguished Scholar Award from the PFDP. The event, which took place on October 30, 2014, was called "A Day of Hope: Honoring the Life and Teachings of Paulo Freire." Our Dean at the time, Don Cardinal, welcomed everyone, saying "Can this world be saved? . . . Days like this give me hope." The event was also special because the president of Brazil had signed into law the directive that "the only existent location of Paulo Freire's handwritten papers and documents outside of Brazil is the Paulo Freire Archive at Chapman" (Paulo Freire Archive Dedication, 2014). Until recently, Paulo had been deemed the Patron of Brazilian Education (Lei no. 12.612).

Nita's presentation that day was an affirmation of, as well as a challenge to, the work that Paulo engendered for the field of education and for humanity at large. His thoughts were neither trivial nor limited to the classroom; rather, Paulo foresaw the extraordinary power of all dialogic spaces to promote challenging discourse, foment critical consciousness, engage in reflection and action, and, ultimately, achieve liberation (P. Freire, 2001). In this paper, I answer the call made by the editors in their introduction to the present volume to accept that text can be a dialogic space . . .

In an essay entitled "Utopia as Praxis: Paulo Freire Twenty Years After His Passing" (2018), Professor Robert Lake engages in a detailed conversation and analysis of the relevance of Paulo's vision for a utopia in praxis across time, something that is perhaps more relevant than ever today. He cites English philosopher Michael Oakeshott to emphasize the importance of dialogue vis-à-vis civilization. "As civilized human beings, we are the inheritors, neither of an inquiry about ourselves and the world, nor of an accumulating body of information, but of a conversation, begun in the primeval forests and extended and made more articulate in the course of centuries. It is a conversation which goes on both in public and within each of ourselves" (Oakeshott, 1962; cited in Lake, 2018, p. 490).

As Nita reminded us of the hope and possibility that lives within all of us as we seek a more utopian world (A. Freire, 2002), she alleges that we can come to realize Paulo's ideas about what it is to seek to be more fully human. We can all do far better in that arena than we have done. Revisiting the words from her speech and her writing caused me to reflect on our present condition and our manner of exploring possibility. That was six years ago, and her words still resonate with me time and again, as they did for many of us sitting in that Bush Conference Center, a space that housed many events contrasting the messaging pictures on the wall of former President George H.W. Bush and his controversial policies. We continue to resist in adversity.

In a world plagued in 2020 by what seemed to be irreversible climate change, we see destiny taking its course in what feels like a response to our many abuses. Mother Nature has sought healing at a time when it seems almost impossible to stop the very political and capital mechanisms that keep pushing the earth toward her demise. In an unexpected turn of events, a tiny microbe, a virus named novel coronavirus (World Health Organization, 2019) caused havoc around the world. It brought the First and Second Worlds to a halt, with the Third World—the most vulnerable—to follow, with unknown, possibly devastating results. The efforts to stop or deter the impact of the disease COVID-19 and the rapid spread of its author, the novel coronavirus, has led us to what can be viewed as a divulgation of untested feasibility.

Almost as if the climate gods had heard the voices of our youth, with

Greta Thunberg (Siddique, 2020) and youth around the world screaming for adults to listen and to help reverse the damage caused by climate change to our world, nature stepped up to intervene in an unprecedented way. And now humankind has done what it thought was never possible: the closing of factories and less air and ground traffic has resulted in a reduction of carbon dioxide from the air, fish are flourishing thanks to the limited number of ships at sea, and people are not driving around to connect with others. Instead they are hunkering down at home and engaging with family members.

According to Corinne Le Quéré, professor of climate change science at the University of East Anglia, "You can see that when governments see there is an emergency, they act straight away with measures commensurate with the threat" (as cited in Watts, 2020). In its reporting, *The Guardian* noted that "The response to the coronavirus could also demonstrate that radical steps can work" (Watts, 2020).

While this has been an incredibly frightening and inconvenient circumstance for most of us, it's disingenuous to deny the threads of a silver lining that glimmer at perhaps the most desperate moments. The birds are singing louder than ever, and we have the time to listen to them. (A mother dove sits right outside my living room window in an abandoned flower pot at this very moment, tending to the needs of her two newborn chicks.) The fish are swimming in bigger schools, enjoying clearer waters in what were prohibited places, and are happily reproducing to welcome spring. Plants are flourishing, many putting food on our tables with the help of humble farmworkers, now deemed our heroes, though ones typically abandoned by our egocentric systems.

Humans in all our splendor are typically very good at neglecting some of the most vulnerable, destroying the very nature that sustains us, and primarily responsible for reducing the potential for life in the future by our inconsiderate and selfish ways. It took one of the tiniest forms of microscopic existence to halt us from further destruction—if only for a moment in time, a screeching halt that has allowed us to look at ourselves in new and critical ways. Untested feasibility means we have the capacity to change; we have the ability to build a better world.

Revolutionary utopia tends to be dynamic rather than static; tends to life rather than death; to the future as a challenge to man's creativity rather than as a repetition of the present; to love as liberation of subjects rather than as pathological possessiveness; to the emotion of life rather than cold abstractions; to living together in harmony rather than gregariousness; to dialogue rather than mutism; to praxis rather than "law and order"; to men who organize themselves reflectively for action rather than men who are organized for passivity; to creative and communicative language rather than prescriptive signals; to reflective challenges rather than domesticated slogans; and to values which are lived rather than myths which are imposed. (P. Freire, 1985, p. 82)

Given the challenge, possibility and hope present themselves, and that possibility comes to fruition to help us get closer to more utopian ideals. A few examples stand out. In a recent post on social media I saw a picture of Venice, Italy, cleared of all the ships that carry large numbers of people, and the water around the city was rich with sea life (Geddo, 2020). In another post I saw a satellite comparison of the air above certain industrial parts of China before and after the viral lockdown, and the results were astounding. What were polluted skies were now clear (Larson, 2020).

It's true that economies around the world will be greatly affected as a consequence of the halt in our normal daily lives, and the impact on industry and capitalistic interests is still unclear. Tragically, we will witness the loss of life in mind-boggling numbers. Is there a silver lining to this crisis? Can we bounce back in a better rendition of ourselves? We are being tested and challenged as to how we might learn and grow from this experience as humankind.

Surprisingly, Elon Musk is making ventilators to address the shortage, as is General Motors (Alexander & Schmidt, 2020). Bacardi rum facilities in Puerto Rico are making antibacterial products (¡Salud!, 2020). Major national and international conferences are being held virtually, postponed, or cancelled altogether, as ways are sought to connect with members this year (Masunaga, Hussain, & Morgan, 2020). Most universities and schools have gone virtual (Jones, 2020). It is a new world, testing every one of us, every agency, every industry, every nation, and every possibility.

On the news, I recently saw the superintendent of the Los Angeles Unified School District (LAUSD) say that the district was spending $100 million to provide computer access to students and their parents. Superintendent Beutner said that "LAUSD was making an emergency $100 million investment to ensure every student is able to access online lessons from home. He announced a deal with Verizon in which LAUSD will cover the cost for the wireless giant to provide internet service to needy families in the district" (Stokes & Javier, 2020)—the impossible made possible. The technology divide has existed for decades, but in testing our human potential and that of the institutions we create, what might have taken many more years to close the digital divide (if that is even possible) is happening in a matter of weeks! Again, in a matter of weeks, education as we know it has been radically changed, though whether or not for the better is left for us to decide. Another bit of good news for many educators, parents, and students is that standardized tests have been canceled in the United States, while free online books are being made accessible, with authors coming to read to children. There are learning games being provided free of charge, and ideas for creativity using simple materials that can be found at home are also being made available. Kids and families in poor communities have access to free meals, and teachers and counselors are engaging in problem solving as teams. It's ironic, and perhaps shocking to some, but everything and anything is possible when people come together. While I'm not one to believe wholeheartedly in the acts of officials from government agencies, they, too, have demonstrated skill in serving the people more effectively.

As an example, the supervisors and City Council of Los Angeles have come together with health providers, industry, and sheriff and fire departments to provide a unified response to the current emergency in the city. In a briefing, each came forward in a non-partisan way to call to action every sector of society to protect health workers, attaining the most critical equipment and medical supplies, and serving the public in an organized and fair way. They worked to reach the most vulnerable populations first in health response (Salahieh & McDade, 2020). Each stood beside the other in support and recognition of their efforts to keep Los Angeles as safe as possible. The National Guard may be called in to work in food banks and transportation. If ever there was a security need, it is to protect the families, the homeless, those with debilitating illnesses, and the elderly in our communities. Despite the professed plan to use the National Guard for humanitarian purposes, military troops of any kind are reminiscent of repression, and this can be worrisome to some of us. This military presence needs to be monitored carefully.

Governor Gavin Newsom of California, who was among the first in the nation to take extraordinary steps to mitigate the virus's spread (NBC News, 2020), stressed that all steps focused on ensuring healthcare were to be taken in concert with each other. His call to provide support to other states and nations was an act of solidarity. To me this stands in stark contrast to politicians such as Donald Trump, speaking in Washington of jumpstarting the economy within a short period, even before it was evident that the spread of the virus was under control (Bartz, 2020). Another stark difference came from a Texas politician who suggested that we encourage the elderly to sacrifice their lives for young people, under the assumption that only the elderly population is vulnerable (Rodriguez, 2020). It is the short-sighted and closed-minded, not the hopeful, who refuse to believe in our potential to overcome adversity in humane ways. This last kind of thinking sounds more like an excuse for genocide than for recovery, life, and health for all. The pushback to that sort of thinking has rallied people to speak out against such heinous thoughts. Instead, people are finding ways to repurpose existing drugs until a cure is found (PR News Wire, 2020).

For the first time in many years, trillions of dollars are being allocated, not just to bail out large corporations (as we witnessed in the past), but to help hospitals, senior facilities, small businesses, and individuals who make less than a living wage. It was a battle of minds in governmental chambers, but they did it (Pecorin, 2020). Perhaps it needed to be more generous to the states, since they are carrying the burden of the pandemic, and to other vulnerable groups. But I expect that this won't be the only opportunity for people to push for tax money to be diverted from other areas, such as the military or the building of a border wall, in order to be directed to the populace; and for more education, science, and health issues. We need to decry the misuse of funds and announce, in a collective voice, the allocation of monies for the purposes intended by and for the people.

The untested-feasibility contains in itself the comprehension of time and space, a denunciation and an announcement. It is in this time and space in which we "patiently impatient" foster the epistemological curiosity that should lead to philosophical and scientific knowledge. It leads to the implementation of the ontological and historical hope through transformative creativity of human dreams. Science and philosophy that do not promote these feasible dreams, and the incarnation of the untested-feasibility materialized in the testing action, do not deserve our respect and consideration. It is not science, it is scientism. It is not philosophy, it is philosophism. (A. Freire, Chapter One herein)

While most societies around the world recognize the need to join forces, innovate, and pool their resources to fight this COVID-19 pandemic, some choose to remain in denial, placing their citizens in peril. Such is the case with Jair Bolsonaro, president of Brazil, who insists on trivializing the impact of this virus (Phillips, 2020). This is the same man who is determined to erase the memory of Paulo Freire from Brazilian education and who denies the vast ravaging fires in the Amazon that have resulted from his careless policies (Bolsonaro to erase Paulo Freire, 2019). This is the same person who won't care for the safety of Brazil's Indigenous communities, a need more pressing than ever. He cannot dream of any semblance of responsibility for the earth's dependence on the rain forest (Waldron, 2019)—the antithesis of untested feasibility.

Needless to say, both this health crisis, the COVID-19 pandemic, and being at the mercy of insensitive and oppressive leaders, are terrible reminders of our vulnerability, requiring us to make decisions that we have never before been faced with—specifically, to make major sacrifices, and to exercise extreme self-control. But it has also been and continues to be a reminder of our potential, our will, and our yearning to be happy, healthy, and free. The time for praxis is now. As Paulo taught us, "Revolutionary praxis must stand opposed to the praxis of the dominant elites, for they are by nature, antithetical" (P. Freire, 1970, p. 126). As Nita Freire stated on that day in 2014, in her pronouncement on untested feasibility:

> It is a word-action, therefore implies praxis. It is a word epistemologically constructed to express—with enormous emotional, cognitive, political, ethical, and ontological charge—the projects and actions of human possibilities. It is a word that brings in itself the germ of possible transformations geared toward a more humane and ethical future. It carries within itself, the beliefs, values, dreams, desires, aspirations, fears, anxieties, the yearning and ability to learn, and the fragility and greatness of human beings. A word that conveys a sound restlessness and beauty rooted within the human condition. (A. Freire, Chapter One herein)

Most nations are making every effort to bring some sense of normalcy to their lives. More importantly, they are focused on saving the lives of those victimized by this dreadful disease that is menacing us all. I hope that they/we can engage in continuous critical reflection and action to further the cause of social justice. This is an opportunity that can bring international accord, economic justice, safety, and a cleaner, healthier world. But it will take ongoing dialogue, vision, and the erasure of personal and societal greed and power mongering. Are we in the midst of what Nita might say ". . . was an untested-feasibility, [that] has now been made concrete and has become a testing action" (Chapter One herein)? As we are reminded:

> Some may think that to affirm dialogue—the encounter of women and men in the world in order to transform the world—is naively and subjectively idealistic. There is nothing, however, more real or concrete than people in the world and with the world, than humans with other humans—and some people against others, as oppressing and oppressed classes. (P. Freire, 1970, p. 129)

Paulo and his living protégé Nita Freire serve as reminders of our criticality in the world. We can continue on this path of testing our potential with hope, generosity, humanity, and agency in building a better, more humane and ideal utopian world. This is not unreasonable. It is not pie in the sky, and we can dare to dream it (P. Freire, 2016). It is a constant reflection and reminder that our actions and reinvention have the untested feasibility to reveal who we are and want to become (P. Freire, 2001, p. 96).

References

Alexander, S., & Schmidt, B. (2020, March 24). *Virus skeptic Musk donates ventilators in what governor calls "heroic effort."* Bloomberg. https://finance.yahoo.com/news/california-governor-says-elon-musk-010555097.html

Bartz, D. (2020, March 25). *Trump says reopen by Easter, corporate America says not so fast.* Reuters. https://www.reuters.com/

Bolsonaro to erase Paulo Freire and feminism from textbooks. (2019, February 12). Telesurtv.net. https://www.telesurenglish.net/news/

Freire, A. (2002). Paulo Freire and the untested feasibility. *Counterpoints*, 209, 7–14. https://www.jstor.org/stable/42979482

Freire, A. (2021, October). The presence of Paulo Freire at Chapman University (Chapter One in the present volume). Myers Education Press.

Freire, P. (1970). *Pedagogy of the oppressed.* Continuum.

Freire, P. (1985). *The politics of education: Culture, power, and liberation.* Bergin & Garvey.

Freire, P. (2001). *Pedagogy of freedom.* Continuum.

Freire, P. (2016). *Daring to dream: Toward a pedagogy of the unfinished.* Routledge.

Geddo, B. (2020, March 18). *The canals of Venice look very different without tourists.* Lonely Planet. https://www.lonelyplanet.com/articles/wild-animals-italy-venice-canals

Jones, J. (2020, March 12). *Schools are rapidly moving to online classes as Coronavirus spreads.* Huffington Post. https://www.huffpost.com/entry/colleges-universities-going-online-coronavirus-fears_n_5e66a6b7c5b605572809cbec

Lake, R.L. (2018). Utopia as praxis: Paulo Freire twenty years after his passing. In P. McLaren & S. SooHoo (Eds.), *Radical imagine-nation: Public pedagogy and praxis.* Peter Lang Publishing. doi: 10.3726/b11176/18.

Larson, C. (2020, March 4). *China's skies clear—for now—while coronavirus shutters factories, empties airports.* Chicago Tribune. https://www.chicagotribune.com/nation-world/ct-nw-china-coronavirus-clear-skies-pictures-20200304-lff4gx-2wlbb5bj7lp4fjbroo4q-story.html

Lei no. 12.612, de 13 de abril de 2012, assinada pela Presidenta Dilma Rousseff.

Masunaga, S., Hussain, S., & Morgan, E. (2020, March 5). *Empty halls. No handshakes. What happens when Coronavirus cancels conferences.* LA Times. https://www.latimes.com/business/story/2020-03-05/coronavirus-industry-conventions

NBC News. (2020, March 9). *Gov. Gavin Newsom and California health officials hold briefing.* https://www.nbclosangeles.com/news/

Paulo Freire Archive Dedication. (2014). Chapman University Digital Commons. https://digitalcommons.chapman.edu/freire_dedication/16/

Pecorin, A. (2020, March 25). *Sen. Chuck Schumer celebrates gains in $2T stimulus deal, says Democrats "improved it."* ABC News. https://abcnews.go.com/Politics/sen-chuck-schumer-celebrates-gains-2t-stimulus-deal/story?id=69789334

Phillips, T. (2020, March 23). *Brazil's Jair Bolsonaro says coronavirus crisis is a media trick.* The Guardian. https://www.theguardian.com/

PR News Wire. (2020, March 17). *Coronavirus puts drug repurposing on the fast track.* Bloomberg Business. https://www.bloomberg.com/press-releases/2020-03-17/coronavirus-puts-drug-repurposing-on-the-fast-track

Rodriguez, A. (2020, March 24). *Texas' lieutenant governor suggests grandparents are willing to die for US economy.* USA Today. https://www.usatoday.com/story/news/nation/2020/03/24/covid-19-texas-official-suggests-elderly-willing-die-economy/2905990001/_

Salahieh, N., & McDade, M.B. (2020, March 23). *L.A. County secures 20,000 new coronavirus tests as 2 COVID-19 deaths, 128 new cases reported.* KTLA 5. https://ktla.com/news/local-news/l-a-county-health-officials-provide-updates-on-coronavirus-response-new-cases/

¡Salud! Bacardí ayudará a producir gel antibacterial ante coronavirus. (2020, March 5). Milenio. https://www.milenio.com/negocios/coronavirus-gel-antibacterial-producira-firma-bacardi

Siddique, H. (2020, February 22). *Greta Thunberg to visit Bristol for youth climate protest.* The Guardian. https://www.theguardian,com/environment/2020/feb/22/greta-thunberg-visit-bristol-youth-climate-protest

Stokes, K., & Javier, C. (2020, March 23). *LA schools are now shut until May—And so far, online learning is falling short.* LAist Southern California Radio (SCPR). https://laist.com/

Waldron, T. (2019, April 24). *"The real virus is Bolsonaro": Pandemic helps fuel Amazon deforestation surge in Brazil.* Huffington Post. https://www.huffpost.com/entry/bolsonaro-amazon-deforestation-coronavirus_n_5ea0ad0bc5b6a486d083a3fc

Watts, J. (2020, March 10). *Coronavirus could cause fall in global CO2 emissions*. The Guardian. https://www.theguardian.com/world/2020/mar/10/coronavirus-could-cause-fall-in-global-co2-emissions

World Health Organization. (2019). *Coronavirus disease (COVID-19) pandemic*. WHO. https://www.who.int/emergencies/diseases/novel-coronavirus-2019

CHAPTER THREE

Untested Feasibility and the Work of Emancipation in a Social Science Classroom

EDGAR OREJEL

SEVERAL YEARS AGO, IN an effort to get to know me, an inquisitive student asked a question that I revisit perennially and had considered deeply before entering the field of education: "Why did you become a teacher?" I remember standing at the front of the classroom and providing a succinct and intentionally provocative answer: "Well, I'm trying to do my part to slow down the decay of human civilization." These words were chosen in the hope that they would elicit an exchange and facilitate dialogue that critical educators dream of. The room broke out in a mix of laughter, puzzlement, serious concern, and universal conversation. Pupils attempted to decipher and give concrete meaning to the selected terminology. I watched groups of young scholars throughout the room begin to discuss war, racism in America, sexism in society, and, at the time, newly elected President Donald J. Trump. As I observed their deliberations, my past, present, and future converged. I was transported back to moments and memories during my pre-service teaching days when my mentor, Dr. Nguyen, would ask me very similar versions of this question. At that time, I was deeply concerned with the monumental task of marrying all the pedagogical requirements of schooling, as defined and constructed by our education system, with my deep personal desire and now life's work to facilitate true emancipatory learning—or, as I would tell Dr. Nguyen in our various conversations and explain to the class—the reason I became an educator.

Emancipatory Education, Hope, and Untested Feasibility

While there are small grains of truth in the question considered with the students, the emancipatory labor that we engage in is squarely rooted in the notion of hope, characterized by an overwhelming faith that if our learning community gets closer to a fundamental understanding of how things are, then we will be better equipped to transcend as individuals and transform the world to what it should be.

When I came across Ana Maria "Nita" Freire's words about untested feasibility (Chapter One in the present volume), I encountered a thought-provoking insight into the concept that would help us bring this notion of hope, in the face of so many societal challenges, to life in the classroom. As Nita Freire elaborates:

> It is a word epistemologically constructed to express—with enormous emotional, cognitive, political, ethical, and ontological charge—the projects and actions of human possibilities. It is a word that brings in itself the germ of possible transformations geared toward a more humane and ethical future. It carries within itself, the beliefs, values, dreams, desires, aspirations, fears, anxieties, the yearning and ability to learn, and the fragility and greatness of human beings. (Chapter One herein)

As a critical educator, Nita Freire's characterization of untested feasibility resonated deeply. This statement is a reminder that facilitating dialogue in a critical learning space that nurtures, develops, and applies this idea and process would touch upon all the attributes of our singular and collective being. We had to be conscientious of this truth and always mindful that hope exists in parallel and in interaction with our principles, ethics, convictions, trepidations, and worries. To this end, as we explored various social science themes in order to understand and assess the world as it is, we needed to continuously acknowledge and honor who we are and what we all bring to our emancipatory dialogue. This would propel the learning community's individual and communal creativity and put us on the path to imagining how the world should be in order to transform it.

Hope in the Classroom

Developing and considering untested feasibilities requires an understanding and analysis of the various limit-situations—conditions and structures that keep much of society in a submerged state of consciousness—that are preventing us from being our best selves and, consequently, stifling the growth and progress of our communities. Paulo's intrinsic awareness of Brazilian society's limit-situations, as Nita describes it, helps us to further understand untested feasibility. Our learning community, like Paulo Freire, must be cognizant of our own society's socioeconomic and sociopolitical organizing principles, as well as the secular conditions of oppression supported by the elitists and authoritarian education (A. Freire, Chapter One herein) that we ourselves encounter regularly. Additionally, we must be mindful that "it is not the limit-situations in and of themselves which create a climate of hopelessness, but rather how they are perceived by women and men at a given historical moment: whether they appear as fetters or as insurmountable barriers" (P. Freire, 2000, p. 99). Within the learning community, we must all understand and work to manage the potential sense of hopelessness by continuously turning to, relying on, and centering our hopes in this critical process.

Unfortunately, the California History-Social Science Framework leaves too many themes and topics in the realm of the abstract and theoretical, posing questions such as "Why do we need a government? How much power should government have over its citizens? What are the dangers of a democratic system?" (California Department of Education, 2017, p. 436). These inquiries disconnect the curriculum from the lived experiences and limit-situations that our students encounter. One only needs to read the news to see that our collective struggles seem to be endless. The inhumane and immoral treatment and detainment of immigrants, refugees, and asylum seekers, the continuing environmental degradation of our planet, and the gender and racial inequities deeply embedded in our society (all of which, by the students' own accounts, have directly impacted their communities), are ignored or kept in the realm of the theoretical in the framework and associated standards and curriculum.

Despite the seemingly endless gloom in the state of global affairs, one can be optimistic about our collective future. There is ample historical evidence to indicate that when humanity works together with compassion and common purpose, we can transcend obstacles and do the work of addressing deeply complex issues. Students inspire me because they continuously exhibit a true and deep yearning to be more than they are. This desire to be more presents wonderful opportunities. Many of us accept the oppressive and limiting elements of society's structures and constructs because we unknowingly (and sometimes knowingly) allow these powerful forces to limit our consciousness and stifle our imagination of what could and should be. The classroom, then, simultaneously becomes a critical space wherein these limit-situations can be analyzed, and a laboratory to develop untested feasibilities, reinforcing old and inspiring new hope among students and teachers alike.

The Dangerous Status Quo and the Global Power Elite

In the context of the social science classroom, the global power elite define and limit our understanding of what could be because they have constructed and upheld sociopolitical, economic, and educational structures that benefit them at the expense of us, the global masses. This small constituency of hyper-rich individuals and families (Mills & Wolfe, 2000, p. 9) is also commonly referred to as the one percent (Elkins, 2018). In the classroom, students regularly identify this assembly of people as the "*real illuminati*"—a reference to the enduring and popular conspiracy theory that a seemingly omnipotent and secretive group is working in unison to place the world under one global regime—whose membership includes an array of figures from billionaire businessman Warren Buffet to the pop icon Beyoncé (Hahn, 2019).

The concept of global power elites was articulated by the late sociologist C. Wright Mills, who showed the interlinking nexus of the social upper class, high-level military officials, multinational corporate leadership, and powerful policymakers (Mills & Wolfe, 2000, pp. 269–283). According to Mills, this group of people control nearly all the major sectors and institutions of our society, thereby dictating and steering governmental policy and public discourse in a manner that directly contradicts and works against the interests and needs of the vast majority of people on the planet (pp. 286–291).

In many cases, these structures that the power elite have developed, managed, and steered are the major contributing factors to the challenges we must confront. To make matters worse, we are forced to participate in these constructions, which can feel demoralizing, stifling, and oppressive. Thus, as critical educators, it is vital that we nurture and facilitate space for students to be able to truly explore, consider, and transcend the current situation that these forces have created. We must adapt the educational experience in a manner that brings about a process that enables our students to think beyond the oppressive vocabulary and language of the global power elites, the fabrications they have designed, and the dangerous status quo they perpetuate. Nita's thoughtful words, again, are an important guiding point to consider:

> Paulo understood the untested feasibility as a strategy, meaning the possibility of taking concrete actions regarding our longings, needs, desires, and dreams socially intended, engaged and realized at every moment by the background-awareness actions, as we approach what actions are historically possible in a given time. Among these, democracy and the realization of Being More have primacy because they are, in fact, the strategy to be achieved, and they correspond to the fulfillment of the ontological vocation of all human beings. (Chapter One herein)

Given these words, by using the classroom as a critical space, we are in actuality bringing background-awareness to critical consciousness. I have come to understand through Nita's words, conversations with Dr. Nguyen, and the exploration of my own philosophical, moral, and spiritual identity, that to be truly critical educators, the way we approach teaching and dialogue must continually evolve. Most, if not all, units, lessons, activities, and teaching practices ought to be designed to ensure that teacher and students think, examine, and dialogue in a manner that places all of us on the path toward developing untested feasibilities. This is where we will find long-lasting emancipation and liberation. This is where our dialogue, learning, and action needs to be centered if we are truly going to do our part to perpetually create and recreate a world where all students have the opportunity to develop the tools and skills necessary to become their best selves.

So, What Now?

Of course, the mission of emancipatory teaching is not simply to facilitate the process of raising awareness about what is wrong or to discuss who are the oppressors and who are the oppressed. We as social science teachers engage in this at various levels, and this is—for lack of a better description—the easy part. The challenge is channeling, developing, and facilitating discourse and learning that embeds untested feasibility—the transformative idea, word, approach, and action that we can, despite the oppression that exists, move beyond our limitations—into units, lessons, and activities. Students are not only engaging in dialogue around the global power elite's oppressive and dangerous tendencies and actions, but also dialoguing, imagining, and constructing new realities that directly confront limit-situations. When the learning community collaborates in this process, we feel discomfort and anger that can be directed into mobilized action. Learning in this space requires imagination. It necessitates that teacher and students identify, consider, and plan to eradicate the oppressive elements of our world through determination, creativity, and action. As Nita Freire states:

> The more untested feasibilities we dream of and materialize, the more they evolve and proliferate in the context of our praxis, in our political wishes, and in our destiny to affirm our most genuine humanity, our ingenious ability to excel when we jump into the fertile and unlimited world of possibilities. Untested feasibility can teach us a wise utopia, into a world of hope that corresponds to plenitude, a seeking of the ontological essentiality of women and men. (A. Freire, 2002, p. 10)

How can this emancipatory dialogue be done in the classroom? How do we discuss limit-situations that have been systemically constructed and perpetuated in the form of global crises? How can we facilitate the process of dreaming and concretizing new, untested feasibilities that empower the learning community while bringing the strength of the global power elite down to equilibrium?

Concretizing the Work in the Social Science Classroom

The concept of untested feasibility is embedded into as much of the curriculum as possible. In our Government class, for example, our first unit focuses on the United States' foundational values and constitutional principles explicitly and implicitly outlined in our foundational documents. This module considers the concept of federalism, the Constitution, and how policy making is influenced by both. The essential questions are modified to invite scholars to think beyond our current structure: What elements of the U.S. federal system should be modified or adapted to ensure that individual rights are fully protected? Which form of democracy would best ensure the preservation of human rights and civil rights in the United States? And, most provocatively, is the United States really a democracy? These inquiries not only compel students to understand our constitutional principles and governmental structure, but also welcome them to think beyond the current reality.

As we progress, pupils begin to define and dialogue about the underlying structure of our government—democracy and republicanism—and our constitutional and foundational principles: consent of the governed, majority rule with respect for minority rights, limited government, federalism, separation of powers, checks and balances, rule of law, natural and inalienable rights, equality, liberty, freedom of religion, speech, press, assembly, due process, and private property. As we explore these topics, students reflect on and articulate which principles they personally believe are most critical for a healthy democracy, linking their own ethics, thoughts, and actions to government and society at large. As we continue to dialogue about which of these principles are in alignment with their own personal beliefs, we add layers of social science content to the discussion as required by the curriculum: ideals of democracy, types of democracy, government power in relation to individual rights, the challenges of the Articles of Confederation and the ratification of the U.S. Constitution, the relationship between states and federal government, and constitutional interpretations of federalism and federalism in action. As students work to develop a more nuanced understanding of the intricacies of the foundations of American democracy—usually about two to three weeks into the unit—we then consider a dangerous limit-situation perpetuated by the global power elite: the continual erosion of democracy around the world, including our American Democracy. This is not done with a focus on particular individuals, but on whether our government's ethics (reflected in norms and traditions established by the elite) and actions (expressed in the policies they promote and codify into law) are in alignment with our own individual ethical code, as well as with our society's underlying foundational and constitutional values and principles.

In order to dive deeper into this limit-situation, we utilize the work of Freedom House, an independent watchdog organization that evaluates 195 countries and 14 territories on 25 indicators related to political rights and civil liberties. Freedom House's 2019 report on the United States is disturbingly titled "The Struggle Comes Home: Attacks on Democracy in the United States" (Brandt et al., 2019). Pupils examine the evidence laid out in the report: U.S. freedom in decline, assailing the rule of law, the demonization of the press, the self-dealing and conflicts of interest, and the attacks on the legitimacy of elections. The young scholars then consider this information by overlaying it with the principles they themselves have determined to be vital to a healthy democracy—equal treatment under the law, upholding due process rights, rule of law, and limited government are popular among the learning community—in order to discuss and consider which foundational principles are being threatened, which threats are of deepest concern, and what can be done.

A Classroom of Hope and Limitless Possibilities

When thinking about the work students have done to connect themselves and their own ethical codes to those of our governing documents and principles, I cannot help but hear the words of Nita Freire in my mind:

> Paulo understood that we are not mere spectators of history that are randomly passing without making any interference . . . reality is constructed by the relationships between our consciousness and daily life consisting of observing, creating, doing, remaking, sensing, understanding, feeling, perceiving, grasping, and systematizing what the natural and cultural world offer or impose on us. (A. Freire, 2002, p. 11)

Nita reminds us all that these incredible young scholars are not bystanders or empty corporeal beings ready to be indoctrinated. They are making history and are ready to engage in the noble endeavor of improving our world. As difficult as this work can be, it is inspiring and thrilling to see our youth consistently show their capacity to engage in the process of understanding their place in the world and, more importantly, improving it. These efforts become contagious because as the learning community dialogues, dreams, and concretizes more, we feel compelled and empowered to do more – *to be more* (Chapter One herein). As our untested feasibilities begin to take hold within the classroom and multiply outside the classroom, limitless possibilities emerge and take hold.

References

Brandt, C., Linzer, I., O'Toole, S., Puddington, A., Repucci, S., Roylance, T., Schenkkan, N., Shahbaz, A., Slipowitz, A., & Watson, C. (2019). *Freedom in the world 2019: Democracy in retreat* (pp. 1–31). Freedom House.

California Department of Education. (2017). *History–social science framework for California public schools, kindergarten through grade twelve.* https://www.cde.ca.gov/ci/hs/cf/hssframework.asp

Elkins, K. (2018, July 27). *Here's how much you have to earn to be in the top 1% in every US state.* CNBC. https://www.cnbc.com/2018/07/27/how-much-you-have-to-earn-to-be-in-the-top-1percent-in-every-us-state.html

Freire, A. (2002). Paulo Freire and the untested feasibility. *Counterpoints*, 209, 7–14. http://www.jstor.org/stable/42979482

Freire, A. (2021). The presence of Paulo Freire at Chapman University (Chapter One in the present volume). Myers Education Press.

Freire, P. (2000). *Pedagogy of the oppressed* (30th anniversary ed.). Intro by D. Macedo; trans. M.B. Ramos. Continuum.

Hahn, J.D. (2019, August 19). *So, what exactly is the Illuminati Conspiracy?* Complex. https://www.complex.com/pop-culture/2018/09/what-is-the-illuminati-conspiracy-and-who-are-its-members/

Mills, C.W., & Wolfe, A. (2000). *The power elite.* Oxford University Press.

Section One: Questions and Activity

Questions

1. In her chapter, Nita Freire, like Paulo, encourages us to examine and analyze limit situations impacting both our humanity and work. In your current context, what limit situations keep you from transformation?
2. Colón-Muñiz gives examples of *untested feasibility made concrete*—work already in progress by activists who are concerned about *economic justice, safety, and a cleaner, healthier world.* In what situations in your context have you seen *untested feasibilities* in operation?
3. Edgar Orejel, with his students, concretizes a communal classroom practice in which they study and contextualize current social, political, and economic deep structures. Within your practice, how can you create intentional curricular spaces for democratic meaning-making?

Activity: Dreaming Exercise

These questions have asked you to: (a) name limit situations, (b) recognize current actions addressing *your named* limit situations, and (c) create intentional communal spaces for enacting change. Thinking about a specific limit situation or challenge you are currently facing, create an action plan for enacting change.

- What steps would you take to address the challenge?
- Who would be involved?
- What outcomes do you imagine?

Section Two

CHAPTER FOUR

The 2RA Method:

Paulo Freire's Pedagogy in Formal Classroom Settings

TOM WILSON

Posthumously Revised by the book editors in December 2020

FOR MANY YEARS, I have been struggling with the problem of how to bring the wisdom of Paulo Freire and John Dewey to bear upon actual, formal university classroom practice. While I never met John, since 1984 I have had the opportunity to know Paulo through attending meetings at which he spoke, and by bringing him to the University of California, Irvine (UCI) for extensive dialogues several times in the 1980s and at Chapman University in Orange, California, in 1992. This latter visit resulted in Chapman University awarding him an honorary doctoral degree, the creation of a bust of him currently displayed on the campus, and the establishment of the Paulo Freire Democratic Project within the School of Education. In conversation with Paulo Freire during one of his journeys to UCI, at a small gathering to celebrate Myles Horton's 80th birthday in Los Angeles in 1987, I asked him who had influenced his own development. He thought for a moment and replied (to the best of my memory), "Marx, Gramsci, Freud, Fanon, Fromm, and, oh, of course, John Dewey."

Freire and Dewey

Freire's body of work reflects Dewey's (1916, 1938) influence first by emphasizing learning through experience and engaging in collaborative work, starting from where students are and speaking in their language, and further, by the rejection of the dualism of theory and practice. However, Freire's cultural emphasis on structural social change in oppressive societies and the condition of both the oppressed and the oppressors provides a critical stance missing from Dewey. Gadotti (1994) states it thusly:

> But we can find a difference in their notions of culture. For Dewey, culture is simplified as it doesn't involve the social, racial, and ethnic elements while for Paulo Freire it has an anthropological connotation as the educational action always takes place in the culture of the pupil . . . , but from Paulo Freire, the goals are different with his liberating vision, education should be linked to a structural change in the oppressive society. (pp. 117–118)

This difference is not inconsequential. I believe the strongest bond between Dewey and Freire is the bedrock belief in the integrative, democratic, and moral foundation of educational practice. Such practice cannot be divorced from other contexts but is inextricably bound to individuals within groups, the community and its life, as well as to the larger society. Decisions for change made in the education milieu are moral, for they always contain within them questions of power and the resultant impact of power upon both individuals and the system. These decisions have moral and ethical consequences for the education of students as moral agents (Frankena, 1980), as well as for the state of democracy itself. Ethical concerns cannot be divorced from the obligation of education's democratic purpose. As Dewey (1888) noted over 100 years ago, "Democracy is an ethical idea, the idea of a personality, with truly infinite capacities, incorporated with every man. Democracy and the one, the ultimate, ethical ideal of humanity are to my mind synonyms" (p. 248).

I believe that Paulo Freire would have no difficulty in accepting Dewey's (1916) integration of the ethical with the democratic, yet by using Freire's often-heard phrase, *in the final analysis*, it is necessary to explicate the notion of democracy from a critical perspective. From this view education, in general, is "one place where the individual and society are constructed, a social action which can either empower or domesticate students" (Shor, 1993, p. 100). An education based on Freire's principles is one that:

> Challenges teachers and students to empower themselves for social change, to advance democracy and equality as they advance their literacy and knowledge. His critical methods ask teachers and students to question existing knowledge as part of the questioning habits appropriate for citizens in a democracy. In Freire in critical classrooms, teachers reject the methods which make students passive and anti-intellectual. They do not lecture students into sleepy silence. They do not prepare students for a life of political alienation in society. (Shor, 1993, p. 24)

Shor (1993), drawing from Freire, writes that "the whole activity of education is political in nature" (p. 27). It is democratic education and education for democracy that are both political and critical. The political permeates all aspects of education: organizational patterns, knowledge legitimization, curriculum content, interpersonal relations, discipline procedures, testing, grading, physical plants, budgets. *Who speaks to whom about what* are all saturated with political and thereby democratic problems and consequences. The task is to pose these democratic problems in a process of naming, reflecting, and acting to transform education into a democratic, critical consciousness that rejects all forms of domination and oppression by recognizing the necessity to challenge repression, discrimination, and inequality, and to speak for social justice (Connell, 1993; McLaren & da Silva, 1993). Thus, as democracy was ethical for Dewey, this Freirean critical task is also fundamentally ethical. McLaren and da Silva (1993) capture this forcefully:

> What makes Freire's work so important for social and pedagogical struggle at this historical juncture is that it constitutes an *ethics of obligation* [emphasis in original]—an ethics going beyond liberal humanist concerns with self-esteem so prevalent in the mainstream pedagogical discourses of capitalist countries. (McLaren & da Silva, 1993, pp. 83–84)

Theory and Action

Eisner (1994) criticizes the proponents of the critical perspective as being long on theory and short on practice. "They are typically more interested in displaying the shortcomings of schooling than providing models toward which schools should aspire in the main, tell the world what schooling suffers from, but they tend to emphasize criticism rather than construction" (pp. 75–76). Yet Eisner cites Freire as a positive example of an educator who "rolled up his sleeves to demonstrate an approach to educational practice that reflects his educational ideology" (p. 76), as did Dewey with the development of his 1896 Laboratory School at the University of Chicago (Westbrook, 1991).

Eisner is quite correct in his assessment of Freire—and by extension Dewey—about the need for concretizing all theory. Freire (1993) insists that our ideas about reality require a methodology by which they can be placed into practice; otherwise they will remain as "alienated and alienating 'blah'" (p. 68). I do not think Dewey would disagree. The question then becomes one of ascertaining how Freire's experiences in Brazil, and throughout the non-western world, speak to those of us who wish to improve educational practice in college and university settings within western contexts.

Richard Schaull, quoted in the foreword to the thirtieth-anniversary edition of Freire's *Pedagogy of the Oppressed* (originally published in 1970), states: "we may discover that his methodology as well as his educational philosophy are as important for us as for the dispossessed in Latin America" (Freire, 2000, p. 9). Discussing this methodology, the publisher continues:

> These words have proved prophetic. Paulo Freire's book has taken on a considerable relevance for educators in our own technologically advanced society, which to our detriment acts to program the individual—especially the disadvantaged—to a rigid conformity. A new underclass has been created, and it is everyone's responsibility to react thoughtfully and positively to the situation. (p. 9)

The pedagogical issue that confronts us thus becomes: What does one do concretely within the confines of mostly traditional postsecondary classrooms to meet the challenge presented to us by Dewey and Freire? It is this problem that I continue to address and explore. A way in which I have considered this issue in my work with students is by using the 2RA methodology.

The 2RA Methodology

Foundational to my work is the Reading, Reflection, and Reaction of 3R pedagogy drawn largely from Freire's notions as developed by Martuza &

Johns (1986). Reading refers to students explaining meaning from any text. Text, in this sense, applies not only to written material but to themes, topics, and even situations that can be "read" and thus understood. In Freire's (1970) terms, one learns to *read the words* so that one can then *read the world*. Reflection denotes the personalization of such meaning, the connections between the material read and the self, the discovering of relationships between one's lived experiences and that which has been read. Reaction indicates the application of the synthesis of reading and reflection to promote progressive social change. It is the move necessary to prevent the "blah" from occurring.

Drawing from Martuza's original endeavors, I have developed a pedagogy titled 2RA. I have maintained the first 2R from Martuza and Johns (1986) but have changed the third R to an A, which stands for Action rather than Reaction. It is a simple alteration, yet it suggests a moving ahead rather than a response to some initial force. It suggests a proactive rather than a reactive stance. I also adopt Roger Simon's distinction between teaching and pedagogy as cited by McLaren (McLaren, 1998, p. 165), in which "pedagogy refers to the integration in practice of particular curriculum content and design, classroom strategies and techniques, and evaluation, purpose, and methods. These aspects of educational practice come together in the realities of what happens in classrooms." In contrast to conventional understandings of teaching as an identifiable method only, pedagogy is a holistic endeavor.

To explain this process, I draw from Democracy, Education and Social Change (ED 605), which is one of six required core courses within the Master of Arts in Education program (MAE) in the School of Education, Chapman University, in Orange, California. ED 605 usually meets once a week in a three-hour time block—although it has also been conducted on a Friday evening, all day Saturday, and a half-day Sunday format over four evenly spaced sessions during the semester. Its fundamental purposes are to (1) increase students' awareness of the inextricable connection between democracy and education, and (2) to increase the possibility of constructing critical democratic practices within their students' own educational contexts. Texts include Dewey's *Democracy and Education* (1916), Amy Gutmann's *Democratic Education* (1987), Horton and Freire's *We Make the Road by Walking* (1990), and Apple and Beane's *Democratic Schools* (1995). Within the ED 605 course, students are arranged in small learning groups of five or six members each.

The first challenges to these student groups are to jointly ratify the course syllabus, determine the course schedule (how much reading per class session, how much time allocated to each text, when will other activities occur), and develop the classroom constitution under which we will place ourselves. Fundamentally, there is a contradiction between the first task of collaborative responsibility for class organization and the second task of asking students to engage in the 2RA process—which is theoretically my idea, not theirs. This dilemma is recognized and discussed during the first meeting of the class. Students are generally willing to participate with the understanding that 2RA remains constantly problematic, subject to criticism, and open to *constitutional* change as the course unfolds, something that, in fact, almost always occurs. The second task is to engage in the 2RA process directly.

The following abstract is taken from the full course syllabus demonstrating a pedagogic architecture. It is an attempt at exemplifying democratic co-construction and 2RA engagement. Thus, it acts as a portal to critical consciousness.

The Syllabus

Introduction: This course, to be consistent and internally valid, will be as democratic as we can make it. It will be highly participatory and challenging, both intellectually and ethically, and student focused. Its methodology includes large and small group dialogue, intensive close reading of textual or other material, role plays, self-analysis, structured experiences/simulations, in and out of class writing, *critical friend* criticism of each other's work, artistic endeavors, and the application of media. Additionally, students will participate in activities designed to give some insight to the nature of their own *democratic personhood* through the use of instrumentation and feedback processes. As well, a pedagogy constituted by Reading, Reflection and Action (2RA) will be used.

Reading (RD): Reading herein means paying close attention to the text. Text in this sense can be anything that draws us to a single word, a paragraph, any written material, a visual object, an experience, artistic work, or as Freire has said, any "object of my attention." Using a written text as illustration, the RD process is as follows:

After a close reading of the assigned text, written or otherwise, complete the following: Prepare a set of discussion notes containing:

(1) critical ideas or messages,

(2) the intent, motive, and position on the subject; what does the author want you to believe, and

(3) your questions concerning things not understood, ambiguities, confusions, contradictions which need to be answered more fully to understand the object.

The number of written notes varies but needs to be sufficient to allow for the small group discussion that follows.

These notes are then discussed in a small group called the Learning Group (LG). The purpose of the RD discussion is to reach as much of a shared understanding as possible by staying centered on the content of the "text" (written or otherwise). RD requires very close reading of the text. For example, in the case of Dewey's *Democracy and Education* (1916), the notes/journals become concise representations of Dewey's meaning, intent, motive, position as understood by you the reader. NOTE: At this point, these representations do not include your personal reaction of Dewey, but it is a response directly to the questions: What does Dewey mean to you and what is not understood? These RD notes, handed in at each meeting, are checked off as being completed, but the instructor does not evaluate, grade, or comment on them.

Reflection (RF): The task of this second encounter with the material is to re-examine it in light of the initial Reading discussion in the Large Group and prepare a new set of notes containing:

(1) new questions about the topic,

(2) new insights, evaluative statements, thoughts about the relationship between the current topic and other previous personal experiences encountered outside of the course, and

(3) speculations of the text's functioning to the course itself.

These Reflection notes become the basis for a second round of in-class discussion that provides for a critical analysis of the material, a linkage to your personal experiences, and to the internal workings of the course itself. As well, the Reflection allows for the development of a Democratic Audit—an examination of the democratic nature and orientation of the classroom, school, or other workplace context utilizing their learning from the course. Within the democratic audit, students are asked the following:

(1) What conclusions can you make as to the extent of democratic processes within your work setting?

(2) What specific evidence can you bring to bear to support your conclusions? and

(3) How does this class contribute to greater understanding of the situation?

The Democratic Audit becomes the basis for a Democratic Action Plan. Early Reflections are usually handwritten in class and then expanded, refined, edited, and turned in as homework at the subsequent class meeting. Reflection papers are about two pages in length, double-spaced, and typed.

<u>Action (AC)</u>: The Reflection requires an explanation of the topic under discussion. The next step, Action, calls students to identify ways in which new knowledge can be and/or ought to be applied to create change in educational practice. The goal is to bring about a more democratic, caring, and just society. This critical step in defining and proposing Action is the translation of ideas generated in class into democratic action possibilities beyond the course itself and usually at the school site level. The source of ideas from Action comes largely, but not completely, from the immediate content and processes in the course. It also serves as a take-home midterm examination. It is an assignment of five to six pages in length, double spaced, and typed.

<u>Mechanics</u>: Weekly, each Large Group submits a single folder containing participants' Reading notes, Reflection papers, and a roster of those in attendance. By the next meeting, student work, along with the instructor's comments, questions, and overall reactions, are returned. Again, both the Readings and Reflections are not graded, but are assessed only as either satisfactory or unsatisfactory.

Student Reactions

It is quite possible that a close reading of the 2RA process raises questions that cannot be dealt with solely through additional reading. This may require dialogue with one's colleagues within the classroom setting. 2RA is a complex process, and students struggle with understanding, in Freire's (1970) terms, *naming*. Because of space limitations, it is impossible to describe the exact and full nature of implementation, movement, additional assignments, assessment of student learning through portfolio construction, and group problem identification and research. However, some understanding of student reaction to the course can be gleaned through the following passages taken from the required take-home final Learning Analysis assignment. The Learning Analysis asks students to *re-reflect* upon their entire coursework and experiences in narrative form.

Episcopalian Private Middle School Principal
"I have experienced some discomfort during the readings and discussions in this class. It was because I was faced with some contradictions in my professional life. Much of what I understood about democracy prior to this course was narrow, vague and almost intuitive. Democracy, I thought, dealt with the governing process. Throughout this course, issues of democratic theory expanded and engulfed a much wider perspective . . . . I will be unable to make any significant decision regarding school (and politics in general) without the echoing questions: Is it repressive? Is it discriminatory? I cannot be neutral in education. To not actively pursue justice is to allow injustice to continue. My efforts may produce few tangible results, but I am morally obligated to try. I am obligated to be an agent for social change. The words *democratic* and *ethical* seem more synonymous now."

Public Elementary Teacher
"At first when I was given the outline for this course I was afraid of the process of reflection and reaction. I thought that I was going to do a lot of writing and I did not really understand the necessity for a written reflection of my thoughts. As I progressed through the class, I began to make connections between Dewey's philosophy of learning through experiences and reflections, and I began to realize the importance of my reflections. Reflecting upon the readings and group discussions helped me to internalize the true meaning of democracy and active learning. The reaction portion of my work was difficult for me in the beginning. I would state that I would like to see a change take place in order to have a democratic classroom; however, I had difficulty actually rating how I would bring about the change. I was frustrated because I had these great ideas and I didn't know how to start. I think that Myles Horton's comment about his work at Highlander and how he found a place, moved in, and let it grow, gave me a sense of comfort that I could just begin with one idea and watch it grow in my classroom."

Public Secondary Teacher

"The most beneficial aspect of this class has been the interactions with the books and class discussions. These have been essential in the articulation of my thoughts and beliefs. I am now aware of the relationships and connections between education, social change, and democracy. I feel much more confident and competent as a professional educator, more able to focus on the direction I want to go with my career, less constricted to simply striving to be a good teacher despite what is going on around me and more energized in working for and standing up for real change where it is necessary. I view my profession as a teacher as more important and essential than I ever have. I feel I have the resources to debate and constructively argue with others. And my desire to read and research in this area has increased."

Public Elementary Teacher

"This class and the assignments have not been particularly easy for me. At first, I had some difficulty with the reading. I always make the joke that reading Dewey was a long stretch for someone who was accustomed to reading *People* magazine. I remember reading the first page of Dewey and saying, "What the hell does that mean?" It took about two weeks, but after that my brain adjusted. The second part of this class that I found difficult was that I began to have an opinion before beginning this class. I felt on a gut level that there were aspects of a democratic classroom that motivated students to learn and enjoy the learning process. By taking this course, I was hoping to get answers. Was there a theoretical basis to my gut understanding? The answer is yes. Once I found that indeed there was theory that supported what I thought, I found that I began to voice my opinion. I felt excited that we had the latitude to express. I am learning in different ways. Also, I was impressed that my group was listened to when we felt the 2RA process was no longer accomplishing our goals. These two aspects of the class created an environment, much like the environment that as democratic teachers we could create in our classrooms to promote democratic citizenship. We, in our groups, were able to respond honestly to the readings and to our opinions about them."

Hopefully, these brief abstracts provide a flavor of students' reactions to the course and its pedagogy, as well as an understanding of its progressive lineage. While 2RA comes from the pedagogy of Freire (1970) through Martuza and Johns (1986), its debt to Dewey (1938) in terms of intellectual rigor, community, experimentation, and reflected experience is consciously paid. Therefore, a course about the relationship among democracy, education, and social change should be organized and conducted in a like manner.

As Dewey (1938) asserts, ends need to be consistent with means. At the same time, democratic pedagogy is rarely, if ever, easy. As Freire (1996) reminds us, "teaching democracy is possible, but it is not a job for those who become disenchanted overnight just because the clouds are heavy and threatening. " (p. 154). While I feel I have engaged my initial question, i.e., "how to bring the wisdom of Paulo Freire and John Dewey to bear upon actual, formal university classroom practice," dark skies still exist. Though far from answering the question completely, my experience with the 2RA process leads me to believe that progress is indeed possible. After any storm, there are apt to be rainbows.

References

Apple, M.W., & Beane, J.A. (1995). *Democratic schools.* ERIC.

Connell, R.W. (1993). *Schools & social justice.* Temple University Press.

Dewey, J. (1888). *The ethics of democracy.* Andrews & Company.

Dewey, J. (1916). *Democracy and education.* Macmillan.

Dewey, J. (1938). *Experience and education.* Simon and Schuster.

Eisner, E.W. (1994). Revisionism in art education: Some comments on the preceding articles. *Studies in Art Education,* 35(3), 188–192.

Frankena, W. (1980). *Thinking about morality.* University of Michigan Press.

Freire, P. (1996). *Letters to Cristina: Reflections on my life and work.* Routledge.

Freire, P. (1970). *Pedagogy of the oppressed.* Continuum.

Freire, P. (1998). *Pedagogy of freedom: Ethics, democracy, and civic courage.* Rowman & Littlefield.

Freire, P. (2000). *Pedagogy of the oppressed.* 30th anniversary ed. Continuum.

Gadotti, M. (1994). *Reading Paulo Freire: His life and work.* SUNY Press.

Gutmann, Amy. (1987). *Democratic education.* Princeton University Press.

Horton, M., & Freire, P. (1990). *We make the road by walking: Conversations on education and social change.* Temple University Press.

Leonard, P., & McLaren, P. (eds.). (1992). *Paulo Freire: A critical encounter.* Routledge.

Martuza, V.R., & Johns, D.M. (1986). *A manual for the 3 Rs: Reading, reflecting and reacting.* Instructional Model.

McLaren, P. (1998). *Life in schools: An introduction to critical pedagogy in the foundations of education*. ERIC.

McLaren, P., & da Silva, T. (1993). Decentring pedagogy: Critical resistance, literacy and the politics of memory. In P. Leonard & P. McLaren (Eds.), *Paulo Freire: A critical encounter*, pp. 47–89. Routledge.

McLaren, P., & Shor, I. (Eds.). (1993). *Empowering education: Critical teaching for social change*. University of Chicago Press.

Shor, I. (1993). Education is politics: Paulo Freire's critical pedagogy. In P. McLaren & I. Shor (Eds.), *Empowering education: Critical teaching for social change*. University of Chicago Press.

Westbrook, R. (1991). *John Dewey and American democracy*. Cornell University Press.

CHAPTER FIVE

Read, Reflect, Act with Tom Wilson

SUZANNE SOOHOO

Working with Tom Wilson

WHEN THE LEAD EDITORS of this book asked me to write this essay, they encouraged me to share some of my best stories about Tom Wilson while extolling the virtues of the 2RA method and its process, which was Tom's signature instructional exercise. What follows is a fusion of memoir and Wilson-esque pedagogy, capturing the man and his unique approaches to his students, curriculum, and the shaping of democracy. I will use an echo format because it is reminiscent of his pedagogy. His greatness extends beyond man and method, as you will discover in my contextualization of his classroom presence and philosophy.

I first met Tom Wilson in 1988 when I was a school principal and Tom was a consultant from the University of California, Irvine (UCI). He was director of the Center of UCI's Teaching Institute. His responsibility at my school was to raise critical questions with teachers about the purposes, complexities, and possibilities of schooling.

Teachers: We wonder why our students are not doing well academically.

Tom: What are the conditions that prevent students from doing well?

Teachers: They don't have good school support at home—illiterate parents, limited English speaking, deficit cultural capital, lazy and poor.

While most consultants might lead the faculty to explore the kinds of extra work we should provide students to "catch up," Tom asked: "Why are they poor? What makes you think they are not hard-working? What is a fair and equitable education?" thus taking the faculty down the rabbit hole of economic and political structures that have prevented people from becoming fully participating human beings.

Pushing faculty beyond their usual orbit of problem solving, Tom gently knitted these knotty questions into the regular fabric of faculty room talk, e.g., "Those parents never come to parent conference evenings, they just don't care." Tom's response: "Have you ever considered making home visits? Why not?" One person described his technique as that of a philosophical gnat: "You knew you just got bitten, and at first, the bite seemed inconsequential until you started to itch and simultaneously realized the sanctity of Tom's questions. Those realizations stayed with you for days like a worrisome bug bite." This provocative conversational approach of asking a morally disturbing question that doesn't allow you to immediately return to a position of ignorance or complacency was effective and impactful.

In Dialogue

It is fitting that this essay is structured in an echo dialogue format, because Tom's and my first publication together was a talking chapter in John Novak's 1994 book, *Democratic Teacher Education*, inspired by Paulo Freire's tradition of "spoken books" (SooHoo & Wilson, 1994, p. 163). Spoken books are texts that try to capture authors' lively, engaged dialogue. A famous book in the talking book genre is Horton & Freire (1990), *We Make the Road by Walking: Conversations on Education and Social Change*. Our chapter, "Control and Contradiction in Democratic Teacher Education: Classroom and Curriculum Approaches," was intentionally designed by Tom, who felt strongly that schools and universities must talk and learn from each other to serve public education. Therefore, it was essential to pair a scholarly intellectual from higher education with someone from practice, an organic intellectual, when making sense of educational theory and school phenomena.

The 2RA Method: Read, Reflect, Act

The 2RA method and process was a modest adaptation of Freire's interpretation of Martuza and Johns' (1986) work *A Manual for the 3 Rs: Reading,*

Reflecting, and Reacting: Instructional Model. In our adaptation, we replaced Reaction with Act to position agency, commitment, and responsibility into the algorithm to explicitly avoid what Freire referred to as talk with no action, otherwise known as "blah, blah, blah" (P. Freire, 1998, p. 30). In doing so, we tethered the question of significance (So what?) to action (Now what?).

This Read, Reflect, and Act process was useful when Tom and I co-directed the UCI Partnership, composed of UCI and 14 school districts in Orange County, California. Partnership events consisted of monthly meetings with invited speakers and superintendents, accompanied by a team of teachers. In the forum, we had conversations about issues facing public education (Read). After a brief deconstruction of the conversation, administrators and teachers would relate the topic to their school contexts (Reflect) and collectively suggest different ways to address/solve problems (Act). Most impressive were collective cross-district action plans that responded to the partnership's fundamental question, "What can we do together that we cannot do alone?" We used the 2RA method in action in a partnership with the superintendents. We read together, reflected together, and came up with a plan together.

We also utilized the 2RA in our teaching. Tom and I translated aspects of this problem-posing process (naming, discussion, action) into our higher education classroom practice of 2RA Method: Read, Reflect, Act. Here is a description of the 2RA method that accompanied our syllabi.

> Select and highlight a passage that interests you. It may be one that you agree with or one that stirs questions in your mind. Cite the author, text, page #.
>
> > Read—Summarize in 3-4 sentences what you think the author is saying.
> >
> > Reflect—Write a paragraph connecting the passage to something you have experienced or something you are thinking about.
> >
> > Act—Write a paragraph on an action that you think should be taken to address the issue you have highlighted. This response can include personal action as well as policy suggestions.

The instructor will be looking for evidence of:

(1) uncovering assumptions about curriculum and schooling

(2) critical reflexivity, i.e., wrestling with issues and topics

(3) alternative thinking and responses to problems and issues

2RA Method and Process

As a means of shared meaning-making within the classroom, we would contextualize the why behind the 2RA method. Our goal was to be transparent with students about the intentionality of the exercise.

Read

"Close reading is in literary criticism, careful, sustained interpretation of a brief passage to determine what the author is trying to say and for the reader to bring one's own thoughts and experiences to bear in order to understand more deeply" ("Close reading," 2021). Tom's marginal notes in his books authenticate the internal dialogue and relationship he has had with text. He was inspired by Paulo Freire, who commented once at a conference about close reading. Paulo declared that it sometimes took a full hour for him to read a single page. He reasoned that if an author had mindfully crafted an idea or sentiment, the author deserved a careful and mindful read by the reader. He reported that it had taken him hundreds of hours to read Dewey.

Reflect

Reflection provides students an opportunity to engage personally with a passage. It invites readers to bring their lived experiences to the table for naming and problem-posing. It is the portal that welcomes organic intellectuals, community wisdom and theories-in-use to come into play. It is the nexus of defining "limit situations," pursuing dreams and possibilities, and the embryonic genesis of critical consciousness.

Act

Tom assumed the classroom was a laboratory for social justice. Addressing social problems and epistemological questions required more than dialogue and conversation. Students were encouraged to examine their socio-political locations to define their spheres of influence from which they invested commitment and agency. In ensuing class sessions, students discussed their passages, shared their reflections, and collectivized their action plans.

Developing Critical Consciousness (Conscientização)

Based on Tom's familiarity with both moral educator Lawrence Kohlberg and critical educator Paulo Freire, we used a conceptual scaffold to help students move from thought stages to action. Tom hypothesized that these conceptual guideposts (naming, reflecting, acting) with accompanying queries could prompt deeper levels of critical consciousness—*conscientização* (P. Freire, 1970)—while simultaneously advancing stages of moral development.

Naming
What is the problem?
Should things be as they are?

Reflecting
Why are things as they are?
Who/what is to blame?
What is your role in this situation?

Acting
What can be done to change things?
What should be done?
What have you done?

The accompanying queries/questions, when reflected upon or discussed collectively, had the potential to deepen consciousness. Although Tom came from a school of thought that magnified self-actualization, he would ultimately adjust his hypothesis to include the power of collective wisdom and incorporate intentional steps of *with-ness* (Hogg et al., 2020) and a *praxis of togetherness* (SooHoo et al., 2018).

The following are a few brief examples of Tom's original theory on the development of critical consciousness. He proposed that three concepts—Naming, Reflecting, Acting—*could move* along three stages of consciousness given the right conditions: Magical Consciousness (Conforming Stage), Naïve Consciousness (Reforming Stage), and Critical Consciousness (Transforming Stage). Note the corresponding parallel to the 2RA Read, Reflect, Act. With thoughtful reflection, dialogue, and new knowledge, he proposed that an individual could transition from one state to another; from Magical Consciousness to Naïve Consciousness to Critical Consciousness. He characterized Magical Consciousness as a condition of conforming, Naive Consciousness as a condition of reforming, and Critical Consciousness as a condition of transforming.

Magical Consciousness	Naïve Consciousness	Critical Consciousness
Conforming	Reforming	Transforming

Here are examples of the three stages of consciousness within each conceptual guidepost:

	Magical Consciousness	Naïve Consciousness	Critical Consciousness
	Conforming	Reforming	Transforming
Naming	The individual denies or avoids problems	The individual deviates from social expectations	The individual seeks ways to transform systems
Reflecting	The individual sees facts attributed to superior powers	The individual sees intentionality by the oppressor, rejects oppressor ideology	Individual rejects oppressor ideology and seeks system change
Acting	The individual accepts fatalism with passive acceptance	The individual colludes and meets oppressor expectations	The individual is self-actualizing while seeking dialogue, system and policy change

Liberating and Haunting

Tom was an attentive curriculum specialist. Every pedagogical decision he made focused on preparing future educators to be creators of a just society. Essential questions throughout the semester included: What is justice? What is ethical? What is fair? To accompany these questions, Tom provided students with immediate opportunities to examine their classroom structures and invited them to question, challenge, and co-construct the syllabus, and to transform learning conditions. For those who bristled at the invitation and insisted that he resume traditional authority, he respectfully asked, "Why do you need me to tell you what to do? Why don't you know what you can do to change conditions in public education? What prevents you from knowing?" These questions were both liberating and haunting.

As students conducted self-inventories to answer these questions, they came to realize they were invited to revolutionize the classroom, to architect a place where future teachers could question the prevailing assumptions about teaching and learning, to experiment with possibilities, and to partake as activists in redesigning more humanizing and democratic learning spaces. Many students soon recognized their privilege in Tom's class, a place that awakened the inertia and consciousness of graduate students, enabling them to move to a new level of consciousness and agency.

Tom's colleagues also found themselves conducting self-assessments when Tom was around. Tom's questions at faculty meetings were morally evocative and disturbing. His soft-spoken approach was misleading because his queries typically resulted in a troubling disequilibrium that made our eyebrows furrow and prompted us to reach for our moral compasses—signs that we were pushing through a mental fog to reveal an under-expressed core value.

Now Is the Time

It is now December 2020, and there is mounting evidence of a groundswell of "wokeness," an awakening of human consciousness, across the world, as demonstrated this past year at daily protests against police brutality and declarations of solidarity with Black Lives Matter. As we witness the carbonated catalyst of people of all colors and ages walking, chanting, and raising their voices together, we provide the needed oxygen for George Floyd's legacy to breathe new life into the restructuring of racist police departments and institutions. This global solidarity provides new air to breathe "untested feasibilities" (A. Freire, Chapter One herein) in the name of a more humane and free world. By reading, reflecting, and acting, we approach this critical work with thoughtful deliberation, compassion, and insightful intentionality to create structures that respond compassionately to human needs.

Remembering Tom

Tom departed the planet earth on December 28, 2019, leaving a rich legacy of classroom practices to evoke critical consciousness. When he came to class, he was spiritually accompanied by his critical friends Paulo Freire, Lawrence Kohlberg, and John Dewey; their spirit and wisdom occupied a presence among us. It is hoped that as you enjoy this book, you will experience the genius of Tom Wilson through the authors and editors of this collection, who are Tom's former students and colleagues.

In my mind's eye, I picture Tom in heaven, engaged in deep dialogue with new and old critical friends, enjoying cookies and milk. He could smell a cookie reception on campus two buildings away. We often scouted those receptions to steal a cookie or two. God forgive us.

On behalf of his students and colleagues, we salute Tom Wilson with a glass of milk and a plate of cookies for his loving gift of disturbing our complacency so that we might more fully act in socially just ways.

We love you Tom.

References

Close reading. (2021, July 21). In Wikipedia. https://en.wikipedia.org/wiki/Close_reading

Freire, A. (2021). The presence of Paulo Freire at Chapman University. In C. Achieng-Evensen, K. Stockbridge, & S. SooHoo (Eds.), *Freirean echoes: Scholars and practitioners dialogue on critical ideas in education.* (Chapter One in the present volume). Myers Education Press.

Freire, P. (1970). *Pedagogy of the oppressed.* Continuum.

Freire, P. (1998). *Pedagogy of freedom.* Rowman & Littlefield.

Hogg, L., Stockbridge, K., Achieng-Evensen, C., & SooHoo, S. (Eds.). (2020). *Pedagogies of With-ness: Students, teachers, voice and agency.* Myers Education Press.

Horton, M., & Freire, P. (1990). *We make the road by walking: Conversations on education and social change.* Temple University Press.

Martuza, V., & Johns, D. (1986). *A manual for the 3 Rs: Reading, reflecting, and reacting. Instructional model.* Center for Instructional Effectiveness, University of Delaware.

Novak, J.M. (1994). *Democratic teacher education: Programs, processes, problems, and prospects.* SUNY Press.

SooHoo, S., & Wilson, T. (1994). Control and contradiction in democratic teacher education: Classroom and curriculum approaches. In J.M. Novak (Ed.), *Democratic teacher education: Programs, processes, problems, and prospects.* SUNY Press.

SooHoo, S., Huerta, P., Meza P., Bolin, T., & Stockbridge, K. (2018). *Let's chat: Cultivating community university dialogue.* Myers Education Press.

CHAPTER SIX

Standing on the Shoulders of Giants

GREGORY WARREN

> *"If I have seen further than others, it is by standing upon the shoulders of giants."*
>
> —Sir Isaac Newton (Gleick, 2004)

TOM WILSON WAS A resonant professor at Chapman University's College of Educational Studies: a visionary educator, academic, learner, and social justice advocate who stood on the shoulders of John Dewey's Progressive Education, Erich Fromm's Critical Theory, Lawrence Kohlberg's Moral Development Theory, Paulo Freire's Critical Pedagogy, and Victor Martuza and David Johns's Instructional Model to bring his 2RA (Read, Reflect, Act) conceptual model to fruition.

For years, Tom struggled with how to extract the light of Dewey and Freire to teach learning communities. Eventually, he was able to blend the epistemology of Fromm, Kohlberg, Dewey, and Freire into his own intellectually tailored epistemology. Subsequently, Tom discovered Martuza and Johns's 3 Rs methodology, which he parlayed like a launching pad to inaugurate his 2RA model. In this chapter, I will be applying Tom's 2RA conceptual model to his 2RA paper.

I began the 2RA process by first reading Tom's paper presented at the Moral Education Association Conference in 1998. After an initial read of Tom's (Wilson, Chapter Four herein) 2RA conceptual model, I paid close attention to the text. I focused on a single word: *democracy*. Tom was a firm believer in a democratic praxis in the classroom. As a historian, my reflection takes the form of a search for the historical intellectual roots of Tom's democratic vision for education, which influenced the construction of his 2RA conceptual model. At the core of this essay are philosophical touchstones marking Tom's intellectual pathways. I end the essay with Action—accepting the Freirean challenge *to reinvent* Tom's work by introducing the ethic of Caring, resulting in a 2RAC model of study and consciousness development.

John Dewey—Progressive Education

As a founding member of the National Association for the Advancement of Colored People, Dewey (2007) believed that a beneficial education should have purposes and benefits for the individual learner and society. From Dewey's perspective, the long-term and short-term qualities of educational experience should have equal weight. Educators are responsible for providing experiences that are immediately relevant and valuable to learners, and which ultimately prepare them to make societal contributions.

Throughout *Experience and Education* (2007), Dewey emphasized the subjective nature of a learner's experience and an imperative for the teacher to understand that experience. With this knowledge, teachers can fuel dialogue with learners, forging a liberating educational experience. Dewey's perspective on experience, education, and democracy influenced Tom's epistemology. Another seminal contributor to Tom's epistemology was Erich Fromm.

Erich Fromm—Critical Theory

As a social philosophy that pertains to a reflective assessment and critique of society and culture, critical theory reveals and challenges power structures. Critical theory was created by Max Horkheimer and his protégé, Erich Fromm. As a practicing psychoanalyst and a committed social theorist, Fromm could observe and theorize individual troubles and public issues simultaneously. He leveraged his religious upbringing and brought a humanistic ethic and a vision of possibility that would contribute to Wilson's 2RA. Fromm's comprehension of the nature of society and human activity paved the way for Tom to stand on his shoulders.

Throughout his vast corpus of essays and books, Fromm (2014) asserted that an understanding of fundamental human needs is critical to the understanding of society and humanity. He argued that social systems significantly contribute to societal, psychological conflicts, and that the implications of modernization could be addressed through self-awareness and critical reflection.

As part of his first significant work, *Escape from Freedom* (Fromm, 1994), Fromm provided a historical rendering of the growth of freedom, self-awareness, and critical thought. Using psychoanalytic techniques, he asserted that the volatile, uncertain, complex, and ambiguous nuanced nature of modernization caused human beings to abdicate their agency and surrender that agency to totalitarian movements. Eventually, his accumulated learning and reflection would lead to the publication of *To Have or To Be?* (Fromm, 2013).

In *To Have or To Be?* presents a compelling perspective in which he asserts that two means of existence are in an infinite state of competition for "the spirit of mankind." The two modes of existence are having and being. The having mode pursues things and materialism through aggression and greed. Conversely, the being mode, forged by love, produces a desire for shared experiences and productive activity. Fromm ultimately asserts that the dominance of the having mode was catapulting the world toward the abyss of ecological, social, and psychological disaster. Essentially, he argued that unless human character changed "from a preponderance of the having mode to a preponderance of the being mode," we would inevitably descend into an abyss of psychological, economic, and social calamity. While Fromm's shoulders provided solid support for Tom's critical perspective, Lawrence Kohlberg's theoretical framework supported what would eventually be known as Tom's 2RA.

Lawrence Kohlberg—Moral Development

After graduating from the University of Chicago with a bachelor's degree in Psychology, Lawrence Kohlberg went on to pursue his doctoral studies. As a doctoral fellow at his alma mater, he became interested in Jean Piaget's work on the moral development of children.

Piaget (2007) theorized that children naturally progress by means of moral reasoning based on the consequences of an act (i.e., punishment), to an action that accounts for the intentions of the individual. Using Piaget's Ages and Stages (1929) theoretical framework as a foundation for his dissertation, Kohlberg (1972) used the responses of seventy-two lower-income White boys as the basis for his six-stage theory of moral development.

During Kohlberg's graduate studies, the topic of moral development evaded exploration by American psychologists. Kohlberg's theory of moral development and his broad pursuit of an intersectional blend of philosophy, sociology, psychology, and other fields of study would influence Tom and Paulo Freire.

Paulo Freire—Critical Pedagogy

Eventually, the renderings of critical pedagogy would make their way to the heart and soul of Tom. Critical pedagogy is a philosophy of the relationship between oppression, education, imperialism, and liberation developed from the work of Paulo Freire (1970). Freire views teaching as a political act that addresses challenges related to inequality. Critical pedagogy interrogates our well-endowed precepts of knowledge. Essentially, the concept empowers individuals to transform the world into a place where they become critically conscious and motivated to change systems and processes. It is the role of the critical pedagogue to work alongside people as they become critically conscious. In this process, individuals unbind their cognitive wrists by recognizing their limit situations to discover new ways of learning and critical thought.

Freire (1970) asserted that schools are part of an indoctrination process that contributes to oppression and supports the activities of the oppressor. This oppression in school settings manifests through the installation of ideas, values, and a curriculum that fulfills the objectives of the government, business, and other oppressors. The irony is that many oppressors are unaware of the fact that they are oppressive. They are cogs in the mechanical gears of a system that intends to control and oppress.

According to Freire (1970), a critical consciousness allows one to have a deeper understanding of the world's social and political complexities. The enlightenment associated with critical consciousness allows the oppressed and the oppressor to utilize the process of praxis for "reflection and action upon the world to transform it" (p. 51). Freire further asserts that when the oppressed have acquired the desire to alter their reality, they will be able to use their critical consciousness to embark upon an odyssey of change.

Operating from the premise that "Liberating education consists in acts of cognition, not transferals of information" (Freire, 1970, p. 79), educators pursue liberation through the iterative process of praxis. According to

Freire (1970), the process of dialogue can dissolve the traditionally complex teacher-student relationship. Freire's perspectives on dialogue and democracy contributed significantly to Tom's quest for effective higher education teaching methods and democratic classrooms. His search to refine his teaching praxis would lead him to become acquainted with the work of Victor Martuza and David Johns (1986).

Victor Martuza and David Johns—Instructional Model

As part of a homeostatic response to the hostile learning environment that emanated from public schools, Martuza and Johns (1986) leveraged Freire's (1998) influence. They developed a pedagogical approach known as the 3R to assist schools in preparing students for a democratic and pluralistic society. The 3R is a pedagogical technique that tends to channel energy and resources in collaborative ways—ways that have a chance of addressing the most fundamental weaknesses of teaching practice. Based on small-group democratic conversations, the 3R method consists of three distinct phases—Reading, Reflecting, and Reacting—that constitute the transfer of necessary skills beyond the classroom and toward lifelong learning.

After ruminating on Martuza and Johns's (1986) work, Tom made a significant modification to the 3R model. Eventually, Tom would name his modification the 2RA and present a paper on the 2RA at Dartmouth University, at the annual meeting of the Association for Moral Education (Wilson, Chapter Four herein).

Tom Wilson—The 2RA Theoretical Model

During his presentation at the Association for Moral Education in 1998, Tom acknowledged that he had been struggling with the challenge of conjoining the philosophical renderings of John Dewey and Paulo Freire and bringing the fruit of that labor into the formal university classroom setting. When Tom modified Martuza and Johns's (1986) 3R theoretical framework, he stood on the shoulders of giants, acquiring a broader pedagogical vista, and creating an amended conceptual framework based on Reading, Reflecting, and Action. Freire (1970) advises his followers not to replicate his work but instead to reinvent his ideas as they fit new contexts and social circumstances. With this encouragement, Tom Wilson adapted Martuza and Johns's 3R model to his 2RA Model.

My Action—An Epiphany of Care

Tom's movement from Martuza and Johns's final process of Reaction to one of Action involved a significant pedagogical and methodological reorientation. This reorientation was philosophically important in ensuring that action was an inherent component of the 2RA process, echoing Freire's liberatory praxis of continual reinvention and remaking of our world.

My reflection on Tom's model included a brief study of the intellectual roots of Tom's fundamental vision of democratic consciousness development. From that perch, I could recognize the valuable contribution of Tom's thinking about Action. Thought and talk with no action was what Freire called "blah, blah, blah." Likewise, action without thought was blind activism. Tom's 2RA model parallels prefigurative democracy (Bolin, 2017)—engaging democratically what one strives to achieve in a democratic society. Enacting the 2RA requires democratic action as an essential response to thinking critically.

Informed by Freire, Tom's process in developing the 2RA modification inspired me to humbly offer another dimension to the 2RA process. While Tom preferred an Action phase of the 2RA over Martuza and Johns's Reaction phase, I have concluded that Tom's 2RA is missing a critical element that is implied but is not explicitly proclaimed in the 2RA. That missing element is caring.

Caring is the element that actualizes, fertilizes, and energizes a democratic learning (Noddings, 2013). Caring fuels compassion for and establishes rapport with people who are different from us. Conveying care and concern for others provides an individual with the capacity to ignite and sustain transcendental relationships. If we are strict adherents to the Read, Reflect, and Act aspect of the 2RA, we will miss out on creating a caring and democratic space for learning. According to Noddings (2013), "It is clear, of course, that there is also danger in failing to think objectively and well in caring situations. We quite properly enter a rational-object mode as we try to decide exactly what we will do on behalf of the cared for" (p. 26).

I stand on the shoulders of Martuza and Johns's 3R (1986), Wilson's 2RA (Chapter Four herein), and Noddings's concept of Caring (2013) when declaring an evolved 2RAC theoretical model. Rather than Read, Reflect, and Act (2RA), I must assert that as intellectuals, academics, and global citizens, we must Read, Reflect, Act, and Care (2RAC). To act without the conveyance of care is an expedition toward cautionary tales and unintended consequences. If one cares without acting, they are merely a spectator (Boyatzis & McKee, 2005). Essentially, caring is the passport that facilitates critical consciousness and thought. As Zig Ziglar states, "They don't care about how much you know until they know how much you care" (as cited in Hogan, 2002).

While I advocate that caring be included as the final element of the 2RA, I would also assert that caring is crucial to ethical and critical thought. Noddings (2013) reminds us that we cannot merely espouse an ethic of care. We must enact an ethic of care. Therefore, I would recommend that the 2RA be amended and referred to as the 2RAC. While the 2RAC would retain Tom's provision of Read, Reflect, and Act, the reconstituted model would alchemize the implication of care into a mandate of care. To break the gravitational pull of homeostasis and arouse an ethic of care, we must establish practices of care.

Tom stood on the shoulders of noteworthy scholars like Dewey and Freire to develop the 2RA. While Tom's physical flame has been extinguished by time, his intellectual and spiritual essence continue to light the way for a pantheon of present and future critical pedagogues. I now stand on Tom's giant shoulders prepared to Read, Reflect, Act, and Care. I am grateful for Tom Wilson and his courage to interrogate the processes of schooling and learning.

References

Bolin, T.D. (2017). Struggling for democracy: Paulo Freire and transforming society through education. *Policy Futures in Education*, 15(6), 744–766. https://doi.org/10.1177/1478210317721311

Boyatzis, R.E., & McKee, A. (2005). *Resonant leadership: Renewing yourself and connecting with others through mindfulness, hope, and compassion.* Harvard Business School Press.

Dewey, J. (2007). *Experience and education.* Simon and Schuster.

Freire, P. (1970). *Pedagogy of the oppressed.* Continuum.

Freire, P. (1998). *Pedagogy of freedom: Ethics, democracy, and civic courage.* Rowman & Littlefield.

Fromm, E. (1994). *Escape from freedom.* Macmillan.

Fromm, E. (2013). *To have or to be?* A&C Black.

Fromm, E. (2014). *The essential Fromm: Life between having and being.* Open Road Media.

Gleick, J. (2004). *Isaac Newton.* Vintage.

Hogan, K. (2002). *Selling yourself to others: The new psychology of sales.* Pelican.

Kohlberg, L. (1972, November 23). *Moral development and the new social studies* [speech presented at the National Council for the Social Studies, Boston, Massachusetts]. https://files.eric.ed.gov/fulltext/ED073022.pdf

Martuza, V.R., & Johns, D.M. (1986). *A manual for the 3 Rs: Reading, reflecting and reacting. Instructional model.* ERIC Document no. ED294159. https://files.eric.ed.gov/fulltext/ED294159.pdf

Noddings, N. (2013). *Caring: A relational approach to ethics and moral education.* University of California Press.

Piaget, J. (2007). *The child's conception of the world.* Rowman & Littlefield.

Wilson, T. (2021). The 2RA method: Paulo Freire's pedagogy in formal classroom settings. In C. Achieng-Evensen, K. Stockbridge, & S. SooHoo (Eds.), *Freirean echoes: Scholars and practitioners dialogue on critical ideas in education* (Chapter Four in the present volume). Myers Education Press.

Section Two: Questions and Activity

Questions

1. Wilson posits the 2RA method as a tool for deep study and initial engagement with the concepts of democratic pedagogy. In what ways could this type of practice transform active participation within your learning spaces?
2. SooHoo explains that the 2RA method has the potential to facilitate development along three stages of critical consciousness (Magical, Reform, and Transformative Thinking). What conceptual tools or methodologies have you used to cultivate critical consciousness?
3. Warren utilizes the 2RA method to identify the theoretical roots of Tom Wilson's original work. In so doing, he traces Wilson's intellectual lineage and proposes that *care* should be a key element of this pedagogical practice. Evaluate the 2RA as a model for reflection. How would you use it? Are there elements missing?

Activity

The chapters in Section 2 explored the 2RA as a pedagogical tool for implementing Freirean concepts within learning contexts. For this activity, re-read one of the chapters within this book and engage in Wilson's Reading, Reflection, and Action (2RA) process. What new consciousness or learning emerges?

The 2RA Process:

- **Read**—to name key concepts
- **Respond**—to relate concepts to self and/or social conditions
- **Act**—to propose commitment/ action in response to issue

Section Three

CHAPTER SEVEN

Comrade Jesus, the Dialectic Regained:

An Epistolic Manifesto[1]

PETER MCLAREN

AS CRITICAL EDUCATORS, WE take pride in our search for meaning, and our metamorphosis of consciousness has taken us along many different paths, to different places—if not in a quest for truth, then at least to purchase a crisper and more perspicuous reality from which to inaugurate a radical reconstruction of society through educational, political, and spiritual transformation. What forces are at work to disable our quest are neither apparent nor easily discerned, and critical educators have managed to appropriate many different languages with which to navigate the terrain of current educational reform. This essay adopts the language of Marxist humanism, revolutionary critical pedagogy, and Christian socialism.

What this essay recriminates in official education is not only its puerile understanding of the meaning and purpose of public knowledge, but its hypocrisy in advocating critical thinking—as in the case of the recent educational panacea known as "common core"—while at the same time publically suturing the goals of education to the imperatives of the capitalist marketplace. The idea of the new global citizen—cobbled together from a production line of critically minded consumers who have been educated to make good purchasing choices—is a squalid concept lost in the quagmire of bad infinity, and will only advance the notion that growth through the expansion of neoliberal capitalism automatically means progress for humanity. Critical pedagogy offers an alternative vision and set of goals for the education of humanity. Critical pedagogy is the lucubration of a whole philosophy of praxis that predates Marx and can be found in Biblical texts. If we wish to break from alienated labor, then we must break completely with the logic of capitalist accumulation and profit, and this is something to which Marx and Jesus would agree. Consequently, we covenant our participation in the life history of the world through an endless struggle that constitutes the permanent revolution ahead.

It is no exaggeration to say that public education is under threat of extinction. The uneven but inexorable progress of neoliberal economic policies clearly provided the incubus for transferring the magisterium of education in its entirety to the business community. The world-producing power of the corporate media has not only helped to create a privatized, discount store version of democracy that is allied with the arrogance and greed of the ruling class, but it has turned the public against itself in its support of privatizing schools. The chiliasm of gloom surrounding public schooling that has been fostered by the corporate attack on teachers, teachers' unions, and those who see the privatization of education as a consolatory fantasy designed to line the pockets of corporate investors by selling hope to aggrieved communities, is not likely to abate anytime soon.

Erudite expositors on why the "what," "how," and "why" of effective teaching understand that it cannot be adequately demonstrated by sets of algorithms spawned in the ideological laboratories of scientific management at the behest of billionaire investors in instrumentalist approaches to test-based accountability. At a time in which exercises in "test prep" have now supplanted the Pledge of Allegiance as the most generic form of patriotism in our nation's schools, critical pedagogy serves as a sword of Damocles, hanging over the heads of the nation's educational tribunals and their adsentatores, ingratiators, and sycophants in the business community.

A New Epistemological Alternative

To look mainly to the European social tradition for guidance in the belief that the struggle for a socialist alternative to capitalism is the monopoly of the West would be to succumb to the most crude provinciality and a truncated ethnocentrism. Thomas Fatheuer (2011) has examined recent innovative aspects in the constitutions of Ecuador and Bolivia. In Ecuador, for instance, the right to a "good life"—*buen vivir*—becomes a central objective, a bread-and-butter concern that cannot be relinquished. One of the subsections of the country's constitution deals with the rights to nutrition, health, education, and water, for example. The concept of the good life here is more than economic, social, and cultural rights. It is a basic principle that "forms the foundation of a new development model (*régimen de desarrollo*)" (Fatheuer, 2011, p. 16). Article 275 states: "*Buen Vivir* requires that individuals, communities, peoples and nations are in actual possession of their rights and exercise their responsibilities in the context of interculturalism, respect for diversity and of harmonious coexistence with nature" (cited in Fatheuer, 2011, p. 16). Fatheuer distinguishes the concept of *buen vivir* from the Western idea of prosperity as follows:

> *Buen Vivir* is not geared toward "having more" and does not see accumulation and growth, but rather a state of equilibrium as its goal. Its reference to the indigenous world view is also central: its starting point is not progress or growth as a linear model of thinking, but the attainment and reproduction of the equilibrium state of *Sumak Kausay*. (Fatheuer, 2011, p. 16)

Both Bolivia and Ecuador have utilized their constitutions to re-establish their states in a post-colonial context and are committed to the concept of plurinationalism and the preservation of nature. Here, the state promotes the ethical and moral principles of pluralistic society:

> *amaqhilla, ama llulla, ama suwa* (do not be lazy, do not lie, do not steal), *suma qamaña (vive bien),* ñandereko (*vida armoniosa*—harmonious life), *teko kavi (vida buena), ivi maraei* (*tierra sin mal*—Earth without evil, also translated as "intact environment"), and *qhapaj* ñan (*Camino o vida noble*—the path of wisdom). (Fatheuer, 2011, pp. 17–18)

The concept of *Pachamama* ("Mother Earth") and the rights of nature play a special role designed to put human beings and nature on a foundation of originality, mutuality, and dialogue, and the Defensoría de la Madre Tierra statute is designed to "monitor the validity, promotion, dissemination and implementation of the rights of *Madre Tierra*," and forbid the marketing of Mother Earth (Fatheuer, 2011, p. 18). Here it is stipulated that the earth has a right to regenerate itself. It is important to point out that *buen vivir* is not a return to ancestral, traditional thinking, but is a type of *ch'ixi*, or a concept where something can exist and not exist at the same time—in other words, a third state where modernity is not conceived as homogeneous, but as *cuidadania*, or "difference"; a biocentric world view that permits the simultaneous existence of contradictory states without the need for resolution toward a given pole, and that conceives of life in a way which is not informed by the opposition of nature and humans (Fatheuer, 2011).

John P. Clark (2013), in his magnificent work *The Impossible Community*, has offered an array of possible approaches to take from the perspective of communitarian anarchism. These include a revised version of the libertarian municipalism of the late Murray Bookchin, the Gandhian Sarvodaya movement in India, and the related movement in Sri Lanka called Sarvodaya Shramadana—the Gandhian approach to self-rule and voluntary redistribution of land as collective property to be managed by means of the *gram sabha* ("village assembly") and the *panchayat* ("village committee"). Sarvodaya Shramadana offers four basic virtues: *upekkha* ("mental balance"), *metta* ("goodwill towards all beings"), *karma* ("compassion for all beings who suffer"), and *mundita* ("sympathetic joy for all those liberated from suffering"). Clark's work focuses on the tragedies and contradictions of development, and his discussion of India is particularly insightful (see especially pp. 217–245 and the eloquently informative review of Clark's book by Sethness, 2013). More familiar to teachers are perhaps the examples of the Zapatistas and the Landless Peasants' Movement in Brazil. Clark mentions, as well, the indigenous Adivasi struggles and those by Dalits, fighting the paramilitaries of the transnational mining communities in India.

Instead of reducing citizens and non-citizens alike to their racialized and gendered labor productivity, as is the case with the neoliberal state apparatus, we wish to introduce the term *buen vivir* as an opposing logic to the way we approach our formation as citizen-subjects. We would advise the guardians of the neoliberal state—especially those who are now in the "business" of education—to look toward *Las Américas* for new conceptions of democratic life that could serve as a means of breaking free from the disabling logic of neoliberalism that now engulfs the planet: a new epistemology of living that has so far not been a casualty of the epistemicide of the conquistadores past and present. We still adhere to the proposition that the human mind lives in a largely self-created world of illusion and error, a defective system of false reality from whence we can be rescued only by the development of a critical self-reflexive subjectivity and protagonistic agency. But we would add that such self-creation occurs under conditions not of our own making. Many of those conditions have been created by social relations of production and the way in which neoliberal capitalism has produced nature/human relations as a total world ecology linked to a racialized social division of labor and hyper-nationalism. Critical consciousness here becomes the inverse equivalent of the ignorance of our false consciousness under capitalist social relations of exploitation and alienation. Hence, we seek a social universe outside of the commodification of human labor, a universe deepened by direct and participatory democracy and a quest for *buen vivir*. Samir Amin pitches the challenges thusly:

> Whatever you like to call it, historical capitalism is anything but sustainable. It is only a brief parenthesis in history. Challenging it fundamentally—which our contemporary thinkers cannot imagine is "possible" or even "desirable"—is however the essential condition for the emancipation of dominated workers and peoples (those of the periphery, 80 percent of humanity). And the two dimensions of the challenge are indissoluble. It is not possible to put an end to capitalism unless and until these two dimensions of the same challenge are taken up together. It is not "certain" that this will happen, in which case capitalism will be "overtaken" by the destruction of civilization (beyond the discontents of civilization, to use Freud's phrase) and perhaps of all life on this earth. The scenario of a possible "remake" of the 20th century thus remains but falls far short of the need of humanity embarking on the long transition towards world socialism. The liberal disaster makes it necessary to renew a radical critique of capitalism. The challenge is how to construct, or reconstruct, the internationalism of workers and peoples confronted by the cosmopolitism of oligarchic capital. (Amin, 2010, p. 24)

Clearly, while we need a new epistemology of *buen vivir* and of Sarvodaya Shramadana to help stave off the epistemicide of indigenous knowledges by means of violent Eurocentric practices, we also need a class struggle of transnational reach.

The learning curve of our politicized youth appears mercifully short, a condition created by necessity more than choice. Few of them doubt the seriousness of the situation that we are facing as inhabitants of our planet. They know too much already, and the question remains as to whether they will use their knowledge to join the fight for socialism, in which they risk life and limb, or decide to give in to the distractions of our electronically wired world of infotainment. As I have written elsewhere:

> Global warming and nature–society relations, imperialism, racism, speciesism, sexism, homophobia, genocide and epistemicide are not independent of the capitalist accumulation process, but mutually inform one another. The youth of today comprehend these myths for what they are—diversions designed to enfeeble the struggle for social justice—and they will never have the same force that they once had. During an unprecedented time when capital permeates lines of demarcation and casts its oppressive force through institutions such as the World Bank, the International Monetary Fund, the World Trade Organisation and the US empire, the young activists of today recognise that they cannot pluck wholeness out of the atomised continent of capitalist culture. They must start anew. The genie of transnational contestation and revolt is now out of the lamp, has identified as an ecological proletariat, and has the potential to alter the course of human history—a history that begins with the overthrow of capitalist regimes of accumulation. Although there is no guarantee that from the conflagration that is capital today socialism will find its redeeming application, there is a fervent willingness among our youth to explore new terrains of contestation and struggle. In the midst of increased surveillance, heightened policing, stop-and-frisk policies on the streets, overbroad gang injunctions, and spiraling rates of juvenile incarceration we see determined efforts by youth who are participating in the US Civil Rights Movement, the transnational lesbian, gay, bisexual, transgender and queer (LGBTQ) movement, in various incarnations of feminist struggle, environmentalism and environmental justice movements,

> and in the labour, antiwar, and immigrant rights movements; we also see these determined efforts in struggles among youth movements worldwide, who are bearing witness to and participating in the production of various countersummits, Zapatista Encuentros; social practices that produce use values beyond economic calculation and the competitive relation with the other, and are inspired by practices of social and mutual solidarity, by horizontally-linked clusters outside vertical networks in which the market is protected and enforced; by social cooperation through grassroots democracy, consensus, dialogue and the recognition of the other, by authority and social cooperation developed in fluid relations and self-constituted through interaction; and by a new engagement with the other that transcends locality, job, social condition, gender, age, race, culture, sexual orientation, language, religion and beliefs. In short, they support a global communalidad. (McLaren, 2014a, p. 159).

If the new generation is to help throw off the chains forged by the centuries-old dogma of the capitalist class, then we cannot leave this challenge only to our youth. We need to offer them hope, but hope at the expense of truth can turn optimism into feelings of omnipotence and can lead to a fatal outbreak of hubris. We need to conjugate our hope with seeking new pathways to justice, despite the grim reality that the odds are not in our favor, and perhaps never will be.

Critical revolutionary pedagogy is non-sectarian and emphasizes ecumenical approaches, attempting to incorporate a Marxist humanist critique of alienation under capitalism into the doxa of critical pedagogy—a move that recognizes consciousness and external reality as mutually constitutive, and asserts that there must be an ethical dimension which gives priority to the oppressed, thereby rejecting many of the "diamat" tendencies that held sway in the former Soviet Union and Eastern bloc countries. Such tendencies maintained that they could uncover a transparent reflection of reality and that a focus on human consciousness, self-management and agency within popularly based social movements was unscientific, and that the central focus should be on social relations of production. By contrast, human agency and human needs are not conceptualized by Marxist humanists as secondary or epiphenomenal to objective social forces. Consequently, reform and revolution are not mutually antagonistic relationships, but must be understood in a dialectical relationship to each other. Dialectics does not juxtapose reform and revolution, but mediates them as a "both–and" relationship rather than an "either–or" relationship. The same is true with ecology and the grounding antagonism between capital and labor, such that class struggle is at one and the same time an ecological struggle, taking to heart the Earth First slogan that there can be "no jobs on a dead planet."

Given the post-humanities attack on dialectics by Antonio Negri and others, it might seem antiquated to look to dialectics as a means of creating what Fischman and McLaren (2005) have called the "committed intellectual" as part of the larger development of a philosophy of praxis. However, critics such as Antonio Negri have abandoned dialectics in favor of substituting singular, unresolvable and non-dialectical "antagonisms" for dialectical "contradictions." Asserting that dialectics imposes internal balances in capitalist society, serving as a mechanism for both establishing and maintaining equilibrium, such critics reject the primacy of the forces of production and the shaping of the social relations of production in accordance with its needs (i.e., the correspondence between the forces and relations of production). As Teresa Ebert (2009) and Ebert and Mas'ud Zavarzadeh (2007) have illustrated, Negri believes that the trans-historical power of the subjectivity of the living labor of the multitude gives labor autonomy from capital through acts of self-valorization and affirmation of singularities. He therefore replaces the proletariat as the agent of class struggle with the multitude, while insisting that capital is merely reactive to the self-valorization of the workers, that labor is in effect a subjective power, and that value is not about economic relations but about power relations. It is easy to see how, under Negri's unfocused eye, class struggle evaporates into a series of unresolvable paradoxes in a world reduced to unknowable, and basically unreadable, linguistic self-referentiality.

The problem with Negri and the other anti-dialecticians is that they reject all forms of transcendence in favor of remaining on the plane of immanence, taking the given social reality as a point of departure (Anderson, 2010). However, Anderson rightly notes that we do not have to choose between immanence and transcendence:

> But we do not have to choose between such one-sided alternatives. Consider Hegel's standpoint, as summed up by Theodor Adorno of the Frankfurt School: "To insist on the choice between immanence and transcendence is to revert to the traditional logic criticized in Hegel's polemic against Kant" (Adorno, *Prisms*, p. 31). In fact, Hardt and Negri regularly attack Hegel and the Enlightenment philosophers as conservative and authoritarian, while extolling pre-Enlightenment republican traditions rooted in Machiavelli and Spinoza. What they thereby cut themselves off from is the dialectical notion that a liberated future can emerge from within the present, if the various forces and tendencies that oppose the system can link up in turn with an [*sic*] theory of liberation that sketches out philosophically that emancipatory future for which they yearn.
>
> Marx certainly overcame the pre-Hegelian split between immanence and transcendence. The working class did not exist before capitalism and was a product of the new capitalist order, and was therefore immanent or internal to capitalism. At the same time, however, the alienated and exploited working class fought against capital, not only for a bigger piece of the pie, but also engaged in a struggle to overcome capitalism itself, and was in this sense a force for transcendence (the future in the present). (Anderson, 2010, pp. 11-12)

Even the illustrious Marcuse in his Great Refusal (his analysis of the predatory capitalist system and neoconservatism, or what he referred to as "counterrevolution") displaces the dialectical quality of classical Hegelian and Marxist philosophy, betraying an incapacity to overcome contradiction in his lurching toward a metaphysical or antinomial (neo-Kantian) posture, in which he vacillates between two poles of a contradiction, poles which he regards as antiseptically independent rather than interpenetrating; at times he seemed tragically resigned to the perennial permanence of contradiction and paradox (Reitz, 2000). Here we can benefit from Marx's focus on Hegel's concept of self-movement through second negativity, which leads him to posit a vision of a new society that involves the transcendence of value production as determined by socially necessary labor time. Unlike the popular misconception about Marx's critique of Hegel—that Hegel's idealism was opposed to Marx's materialism—Marx did not criticize Hegel for his failure to deal with material reality. When Marx noted that Hegel knows only abstractly spiritual labor, he was referring to the structure of Hegel's *Phenomenology* and philosophy as a whole, which was based on a dialectic of self-consciousness, in which thought returns to itself by knowing itself (Hudis, 2012). Marx's concept of transcendence, on the contrary, was grounded in human sensuousness, in the self-transcendence of the totality of human powers. Dialectics deals with the transformative contradictions that power the material historicity of capitalist life.

Hegel presented the entire movement of history in terms of the unfolding of the disembodied idea; in other words, he presented human actuality as a product of thought instead of presenting thought as the product of human actuality. Marx, therefore, inverts the relations of Hegel's subject and predicate. Marx criticized Hegel for failing to distinguish between labor as a trans-historical, creative expression of humanity's "species being" and labor as the reduction of such activity to value production. We need to understand the dialectic, the description of the means by which reality unfolds, the nature of self-activity, self-development and self-transcendence, and the way that human activity subjectively and temporally mediates the objective world.

The presence of the idea—as negation—in human consciousness has the power to alter the natural world. Marx was not interested in the returning of thought to itself in Hegel's philosophy, but the return of humanity to itself by overcoming the alienation of the objective world brought about by capitalist social relations. In other words, the human being is the agent of the Idea; the Idea is not its own agent. The human being is the medium of the Idea's self-movement. Self-movement is made possible through the act of negation by negating the barriers to self-development. But negation, as Peter Hudis (2012, pp. 72–73) tells us, is always dependent on the object of its critique. Whatever you negate still bears the stamp of what has been negated—that is, it still bears the imprint of the object of negation. We have seen, for instance, in the past, that oppressive forms which one has attempted to negate still impact the ideas we have of liberation. That is why Hegel argued that we need a self-referential negation—a negation of the negation. By means of a negation of the negation, negation establishes a relation with itself, freeing itself from the external object it is attempting to negate. Because it exists without a relationship to another outside of itself, it is considered to be absolute—it is freed from dependency on the other. It negates its dependency through a self-referential act of negation. For example, the abolition of private property and its replacement with collective property does not ensure liberation; it is only an abstract negation which must be negated in order to reach liberation. It is still infected with its opposite, which focuses exclusively on property. It simply replaces private property with collective property and is still impacted by the idea of ownership or having (Hudis, 2012, pp. 71–73). Hudis writes:

> [Marx] appropriates the concept of the "negation of the negation" to explain the path to a new society. Communism, the abolition of private property, is the negation of capitalism. But this negation, Marx tells us, is dependent on the object of its critique insofar as it replaces private property with collective property. Communism is not free from the alienated notion that ownership or having is the most important part of being human; it simply affirms it on a different level. Of course, Marx thinks that it is necessary to negate private property. But this negation, he insists, must itself be negated. Only then can the truly positive—a totally new society—emerge. As Dunayevskaya writes in P&R [*Philosophy and Revolution*], "The overcoming of this 'transcendence," called absolute negativity by Hegel, is what Marx considered the only way to create a truly human world, 'positive Humanism, beginning from itself.'" (Hudis, 2005, p. 54)

However, in order to abolish capital, the negation of private property must itself be negated, which would be the achievement of a positivity—a positive humanism—beginning with itself. While it is necessary to negate private property, that negation must itself be negated. If you stop before this second negation, then you are presupposing that having is more important than being (Hudis, 2012). Saying "no" to capital, for instance, constitutes a first negation. When the subject becomes self-conscious regarding this negation—that is, when the subject understanding the meaning of this negation recognizes the positive content of this negation—then she has arrived at the negation of the negation. In other words, when a subject comes to recognize that she is the source of the negative, this becomes a second negation, a reaching of class consciousness. When a subject recognizes the positivity of the act of negation itself as negativity, then she knows herself as a source of the movement of the real. This occurs when human beings, as agents of self-determination, hear themselves speak, and are able both to denounce oppression and the evils of the world and to announce, in Freire's terms, a liberating alternative. I fully agree with Reitz (2000, p. 263) that critical knowledge "is knowledge that enables the social negation of the social negation of human life's core activities, the most central of which are neither being-toward-death [as Heidegger would maintain], nor subservience [as Kant would argue], but creative labor." When subjects create critical knowledge, they then are able to appropriate freedom itself for the sake of the liberation of humanity (Pomeroy, 2004).

Searching for an alternative to capitalism means mining the dynamic potentiality that is latent, but unrealized, in everyday life and, in this regard, is redolent of a spiritual quest in the manner suggested by Robert M. Torrance (1994). It requires a deliberate and urgent effort by teachers and teacher educators to transcend, through self-transformation, the limits of everyday reality and the human condition under capitalism, and a willingness to marshal this unbounded potentiality in the direction of social justice. It means realizing the enlarging and transformative potential of the given through a pursuit of the liberation of our collective humanity, a humanity that transcends the individual self not by seeking refuge in an immutable past or inertial present, but by advancing from subjective knowledge to the independently and objectively real that is always oriented to the determinable, living future—a knowledge that is the product of the human mind yet transcends the mind; a knowledge gleaned from the particular through its relationship to the universal; a knowledge that can never be fully apprehended; a knowledge engendered by the seeker yet at the same time transcending the seeker.

We must open our lexicon of critique and transformation to a changing world. As Marx pointed out, any viable exercise of protagonistic agency among the oppressed requires the dialectical self-negation of the working class as a class in itself into a class for itself, a class in which it is imperative to become self-conscious of how its membership is embedded in relations of exploitation and how they have become alienated from their own "species being" or their own life activity. Of course, the overall purpose of this critical transformation is to become emancipated from labor's value form.

We cannot know what the alternative to capitalist value production will look like until the struggle moves forward and we are able to claim some decisive victories. Only then can we know how we will proceed in forging a new alternative to capitalist commodity production. What is clear is that we must dissemble the self-referential closure of the capitalist trance state in which we find ourselves hopelessly enthralled. Through our passive exposure to electronic media, we willfully submit ourselves to the rituals of everyday capitalist commodity production, to their formulaic and habituated repetitiveness and invariance, to their inert sufferance and wearisome recurrence of stasis—all of which ineluctably and fatally disciplines us to assent uncritically to our own acedia and torpor. The only way out of this impasse is to seek an alternative social universe to that of value production.

This involves a pursuit, despite the fact that the goal can never be fully foreknown or finally attained. There is room for all at the banquet of liberation: trade unionists, civil libertarians, anarchists, students, anti-war activists, Marxists, black and Latino activists, teachers, eco-socialists, fast-food workers, factory workers, and animal rights activists. We seek to replace instrumental reason with critical rationality, fostering popular dissent and creating workers' and communal councils and community decision-making structures.

We continue to struggle in our educational projects to eliminate rent-seeking and for-profit financial industries; we seek to distribute incomes without reference to individual productivity, but rather according to need; and we seek to substantially reduce hours of labor and make possible, through socialist general education, a well-rounded and scientific and intercultural development of the young (Reitz, 2013). This involves a larger epistemological fight against neoliberal and imperial common sense, and a grounding of our critical pedagogy in a concrete universal that can welcome diverse and particular social formations (San Juan, 2007) joined in class struggle. It is a struggle that has come down to us not from the distant past, but from thoughts that have ricocheted back to us from the future.

Life does not unfold as some old sheet strewn across a brass bed in the dusky attic of history; our destinies as children, parents, and teachers do not flow unilaterally toward a single vertigo-inducing epiphany, some pyrotechnic explosion of iridescent and refulgent splendor where we lay becalmed, rocking on a silent sea of pure bliss, or where we are held speechless in some wind-washed grove of cedars, happily in the thrall of an unbridled, unsullied, and undiluted love of incandescent intensity. Our lives are not overseen by a handsome God who blithely sits atop a terra cotta pedestal and with guileless simplicity, quiet paternalism, and unsmiling earnestness rules over his eager and fumbling brood, ever so often rumpling the curly heads of the rosy-cheeked cherubim and engaging the saints in blissful conversation about quantum theory. Were there such a God, wrapped in the mantle of an otherworldly Platonism and possessing neither moral obliquity nor guilt, who brings forth the world through supernatural volition alone, the world would be nothing but an echo of the divine mind. Hunger could be ended by merely thinking of a full belly and sickness eliminated by a picture of perfect health.

Most of us, however, sling ourselves nervously back and forth across the great Manichean divide of the drab of everyday existence, where, in our elemental contact with the world, our human desires, for better or for worse, tug at us like some glow-in-the-dark hustler in a carnival midway. We go hungry, we suffer, and we live in torment and witness most of the world's population crumpled up in pain. We don't have to witness a final miracle of eschatological significance to reclaim the world. What we do have to accomplish at this very moment is organizing our world to meet the basic needs of humanity.

Christian Communism Reborn?

But the same message of meeting the needs of humanity was prevalent in the Bible, and occupied the message of Jesus. I do not suddenly mention this out of some otherworldly penchant, but for a concern for the here and the now. The majority of American citizens are Christians of some denomination or other, and it is important to point out as an incontrovertible fact that the message of Jesus in the Gospels is focused on the liberation of the poor from captivity and oppression, thus in Luke 4:18–19: "The Spirit of the Lord is upon me, because he has anointed me to preach good news to the poor. He has sent me to proclaim release to the captives and recovering of sight to the blind, to set at liberty those who are oppressed, to proclaim the acceptable year of the Lord." Jesus was very much opposed to oppression and bondage, and it was no secret that he excluded the wealthy from the kingdom of God, noted in this very clear passage from Matthew 19:16–24 (this authentic logion of Jesus is also described in Mark 10:17–25 and Luke 18:18–25):

> And, behold, one came and said unto him, Good Master, what good thing shall I do, that I may have eternal life? And he said unto him, Why do you ask me about what is good? there is none good

> but one, that is, God: but if thou wilt enter into life, keep the commandments. He saith unto him, Which? Jesus said, Thou shalt do no murder, Thou shalt not commit adultery, Thou shalt not steal, Thou shalt not bear false witness, Honor thy father and thy mother: and, Thou shalt love thy neighbour as thyself. The young man saith unto him, All these things have I kept from my youth up: what lack I yet? Jesus said unto him, If thou wilt be perfect, go and sell that thou hast, and give to the poor, and thou shalt have treasure in heaven: and come and follow me. But when the young man heard that saying, he went away sorrowful: for he had great possessions. Then said Jesus unto his disciples, Verily I say unto you, That a rich man shall hardly enter into the kingdom of heaven. And again I say unto you, It is easier for a camel to go through the eye of a needle, than for a rich man to enter into the kingdom of God.

Many of us—either openly or secretly—harbor a religious faith that often remains hidden between the lines of our manifestos and treatises. I have often maintained the position that the official church of Jesus has been implicated in the indefensible falsification of the gospel in order to protect the hierarchies of the church. But here I wish to amplify this idea by briefly summarizing the important work of José Porfirio Miranda. Miranda's work skillfully corroborates his own analysis of the Bible with those of ecclesiastically sanctioned studies by recognized and prominent Catholic exegetes. According to Miranda (1977, p. 203), Christian faith is supposed to "transform humankind and the world." Miranda (1980; 2004) claims the persecution of Christians for the first three centuries constrained Christians to present a version of Christianity that would no longer provoke repression. After the fourth century, the church acquired a dominant status in class society, and this was what then motivated the continuing falsification of the gospel.

The official teachings of the church falsify the gospel, since it is clear from reading the texts of the Bible that Jesus maintains an intransigent condemnation of the rich. Even liberation theology gets this wrong when it asserts that there should be a "preferential option for the poor"—it is not an option, but, as Miranda notes, it is an obligation. We cannot shirk this obligation without imputation of culpability and still remain Christians. There is no abstention from this struggle. The condition of the poor obliges a restitution, since such a struggle is injustice writ large. Jesus died for participating in political transgression aimed at liberating Judea from the Romans. According to Miranda, Jesus clearly was a communist, and this can be seen convincingly throughout the New Testament, but particularly in passages such as John 12:6, 13:29, and Luke 8:1–3. Jesus went so far as to make the renunciation of property a condition for entering the kingdom of God. When Luke says, "Happy the poor, for yours is the Kingdom of God" (Luke 6:20) and adds, "Woe to you the rich, because you have received your comfort" (Luke 6:24), Luke is repeating Mark 10:25, when Jesus warns that the rich cannot enter the kingdom. The Bible makes clear through Jesus' own sayings that the kingdom is not the state of being after death; rather, the kingdom is now, here on earth. Essentially Jesus is saying that "in the kingdom there cannot be social differences—that the kingdom, whether or not it pleases the conservatives, is a classless society" (Miranda, 2004, p. 20). Consider what Luke says in Acts:

> All the believers together had everything in common; they sold their possessions and their goods, and distributed among all in accordance with each one's need. [Acts 2: 44-45]
>
> The heart of the multitude of believers was one and their soul was one, and not a single one said anything of what he had was his, but all things were in common . . . . There was no poor person among them, since whoever possessed fields or houses sold them, bore the proceeds of the sale and placed them at the feet of the apostles; and a distribution was made to each in accordance with his need. [Acts 4:32, 34–35]

Jesus did not say that the poor will always be with us; he said that the poor are with us all the time. Miranda (2004, pp. 58–60) cites numerous translation sources attesting that this statement should be translated as "The poor you have with you at all moments [or continuously]. And you can do them good when you wish; on the other hand, you do not have me at all moments [Mark 14:7]." According to Miranda (2004, p. 65), Jesus didn't say "my kingdom is not of this world"; he said "my kingdom does not come forth from this world" or "my kingdom is not from this world," since we can retain the original meaning only if we consider the preposition "ek" in the original Greek as meaning "from," signifying place of origin or provenance. But didn't Jesus advocate paying taxes? Rendering unto Cesar what is due Cesar? Jesus's remark about giving Cesar what is due Cesar is decidedly ironic, and not a capitulation to Roman authority (Miranda, 2004, 61–65). Consider the following quotation cited by Miranda (2004, p. 53) concerning economic transactions found in the Bible:

> For the sake of profit, many have sinned; the one who tries to grow rich, turns away his gaze. Stuck tight between two stones, between sale and purchase, sin is wedged. [Ecclus. 27: 1–2]

Miranda (2004, p. 54) notes that Biblical scripture condemns the term "interest" (the Hebrew word is "neshet") numerous times: Exodus 22:24; Leviticus 25:36, 37; Deuteronomy 23:19 (three times); Ezekiel 18:8, 13, 17, 22:12; Psalms, 15:5; Proverbs 28:8. And numerous times profit-making through commerce, loans at interest, and productive activity itself (the process of production) is condemned (production likely here referring to agriculture). Does not James condemn the acquisition of wealth by agricultural entrepreneurs (see James 5:1–6)? And does he not, in fact, attack all the rich (James 1:10–11)? In James 2:6 does he not say: "Is it not the rich who oppress you and who hail you before the tribunals?" Does he not also say: "See, what you have whittled away from the pay of the workers who reap your fields cries out, and the anguish of the harvesters has come to the ears of the Lord of Armies" (James 5:4)? Does it now surprise us that Jesus would call money, "money of iniquity" (Luke 16:9, 11)? On this issue Miranda (2004, p. 55) writes:

> What this verse is doing is explaining the origin of wealth. Its intention is not to refer to *some* particularly perverse rich people who have committed knaveries which other rich people do not commit. The letter's attack is against *all* the rich.

This is the biblical reprobation of differentiating wealth as Luke vituperates those who have defrauded workers and impugns all the rich. According to Miranda (2004, p. 53), profit "is considered to be the source of (differentiating) wealth." Miranda continues:

> For James, differentiating wealth can be acquired only by means of expropriation of the produce of the workers' labor. Therefore,

> following Jesus Christ and the Old Testament, James condemns differentiating wealth without vacillation or compromise. Profit made in the very process of production is thus specifically imprecated. (2004, p. 55)

Miranda (2004, p. 73) explains further what this implies: "Where there is no differentiating wealth, where economic activity is directly for the purpose of the satisfaction of needs and not for trade or the operations of buying and selling for profit, government becomes unnecessary." The Bible attacks not only acquired wealth but the means by which such wealth is accumulated, which is the taking of profit or what could be considered a form of systemic or legalized exploitation. Even the prophets such as Micha and Amos understood that "no differentiating wealth can be acquired without spoliation and fraud" (Miranda, 2004, p. 40). Miranda notes: "If we want to know 'Why communism?' the response is unequivocal: because any other system consists in the exploitation of some persons over others" (2004, p. 55). Miranda sees Jesus as the true God grounded in himself, meaning grounded in the establishment of justice and life now, at this very moment, since "the hour is coming and it is now." Miranda is uncompromising when he notes:

> A god who intervenes in history to elicit religious adoration of himself and not to undo the hell of cruelty and death that human history has become is an immoral god in the deepest sense of the word. A god who is reconciled or merely indifferent to the pain of human beings is a merciless god, a monster, not the ethical God whom the Bible knows. We would be morally obliged to rebel against such a god, even if our defeat were inevitable. Equally immoral is the god for whom the end of injustice and innocent suffering is a secondary or subordinate imperative. (1977, p. 187)

The key point in Miranda's theological argument is that the eschaton has already arrived, the eschaton of justice and life for all, in the example of Jesus Christ. If Christians don't believe that the eschaton has already come, then they are likely to relegate Jesus to a nontemporal and eternal or Platonic realm. But the eschaton cannot be indefinitely held captive in some mythic future; the historical moment of salvation is not repeatable since

Jesus is the divine singularity—the definitive "now" of history. If this were not the case, "then the imperative of love of neighbor becomes an intro-self concept. It does not speak as a real otherness, because anodyne time, even if it is present, truly has no reason to command me more than any other time" (Miranda, 1977, p. 192). Christians can't postpone the commandment to love their neighbor in the fathomless future, because this would make God an unassimilable otherness, a perpetual language game in which postmodernists would love to participate without a commitment to any political imperative except narcissistic self-cultivation. And thus we could never be contemporaneous with God. Eternal life is not life after death but the defeat of death, that is, the defeat of suffering and injustice in the here and now. Of course, what should be condemned are the totalitarian police states that *claimed* to be communist (such as the Soviet Union) but which were, in the final instance, formations of state capitalism (see Dunayevskaya, 1992).

Jesus was likely no quietist who publicly repudiated his Messianic role, avoided political involvement, and rejected the idea of leading a nationalist movement against the Romans. What is clear is that he was executed for sedition at the hands of the Romans, and if he were not a Zealot, then it is likely he was sympathetic to many of their principles (Brandon, 1967). For those Christians—especially the prosperity evangelicals who are so popular in the United States—who promote capitalism and equate faith with wealth, it would serve them well to reconsider their interpretation of the gospels and to consider the fact that communism predated Karl Marx through the teaching of the Bible.

Speaking of the here and now, at the time of this writing residents of Detroit who have not paid their water bills have had their water supply shut off by the city, affecting more than 40% of the customers of the Detroit Water and Sewage Department, and posing a serious health hazard for 200,000–300,000 residents. Detroit is not Cochabamba, Bolivia, in 2000, when protests broke out after a new firm, Aguas del Tunari (involving the Bechtel corporation) invested in the construction of a dam and tried to pay for it by dramatically raising water rates on the local people. A community coalition, Coordinadora in Defense of Water and Life, organized a massive protest movement that finally reversed the privatization. Protests by the people of Detroit have not yet forced the city to keep the water flowing to those who cannot afford their water bills. Is this so surprising? The United States has a history of ignoring the basic needs of its population. William Blum (2014a, p. 54) writes:

> On December 14, 1981, a resolution was proposed in the United Nations General Assembly which declared that "education, work, health care, proper nourishment, national development are human rights." Notice the "proper nourishment." The resolution was approved by a vote of 135–1. The United States cast the only "No" vote.
>
> A year later, December 18, 1982, an identical resolution was proposed in the General Assembly. It was approved by a vote of 131–1. The United States cast the only "No" vote.
>
> The following year, December 16, 1983, the resolution was again put forth, a common practice at the United Nations. This time it was approved by a vote of 132–1. There's no need to tell you who cast the sole "No" vote.
>
> These votes took place under the Reagan administration.
>
> Under the Clinton administration, in 1996, a United Nations-sponsored World Food Summit affirmed the "right of everyone to have access to safe and nutritious food." The United States took issue with this, insisting that it does not recognize a "right to food." Washington instead championed free trade as the key to ending the poverty at the root of hunger, and expressed fears that recognition of a "right to food" could lead to lawsuits from poor nations seeking aid and special trade provisions.
>
> The situation of course did not improve under the administration of George W. Bush. In 2002, in Rome, world leaders at another UN-sponsored World Food Summit again approved a declaration that everyone had the right to "safe and nutritious food." The United States continued to oppose the clause, again fearing it would leave them open to future legal claims by famine-stricken countries.
>
> I'm waiting for a UN resolution affirming the right to oxygen.

No matter how strained we may become in fathoming the calamity of capitalist globalization and its attending antagonisms, we cannot banish these harrowing realities or thrust them out of mind by taking refuge in our books, our theories, our seminar rooms, or in the salons of our organizing committees. We have, after all, a new era to proclaim. Here educators committed to social transformation through incremental means can take heed from the words of Miranda:

> The true revolutionary abjures reformist palliatives, because these divert the efforts of the people most capable of fomenting rebellion against the bourgeois system into rejuvenating and refurbishing it; such palliatives thus constitute the system's best defense. By the same token, the revolutionary must find any change in the socioeconomic system to be a priori inadequate, if that change does not involve a radical revolution in people's attitudes towards each other. If exchange-value (that "imaginary entity") and the desire for personal gain continue to exist, they will inevitably create other oppressive and exploitative economic systems. (1977, pp. 21–22)

The revolution is now. It's the dialectic regained, it's the people unchained, it's the eschaton made immanent. The teachings of Jesus enfold the world in a new community of justice-seeking revolutionaries. While some might dismiss Jesus as an amalgam of myths spawned in the depths of the Mediterranean imagination, the teachings of Jesus inspire us to turn toward the world and create a society of freely associated producers related in profound mutuality and overflowing love. We find our praxis of universal solidarity in suffering and hope and in our collective recognition that we are not alone but exist in the world with others. We recognize the presence of Jesus in the poor and the oppressed, and our response to the call of the other is not an option but an obligation. Early followers of Jesus lived communally, shared their resources, held all property in common, and engaged in a communist lifestyle and held onto communist ideals where goods were distributed "from each according to ability to each according to need" (Rivage-Seul, 2014). Miranda is correct when he writes that truth and imperative are identical; that to abide in the truth means to fight for justice and equality and by making the eschaton immanent. In this way we judge the authenticity of our lives by the criterion of meeting the needs of others, in the historical (and not simply existential) imperative of loving our neighbor. Our task is to understand how to organize ourselves the day after we rid ourselves of the birthmarks of capitalism, of a world in which every social gain must be sacrificed at the altar of profit. Will we be able to project a viable alternative to the dominance of capital? How can we avoid the horrors of existing capitalist society in our attempt to replace it with a socialist alternative? How can we avoid the terror of societies that existed in places such as the former Soviet Union that destroyed the soviets (workers' councils) and replaced them with a totalitarian dictatorship that suppressed communism and replaced it with state capitalism? How can we prevent ourselves from descending into a narrow nationalism? How can we fully reclaim the biblical roots of communism that can be found in the Acts of the Apostles? How can we reclaim Jesus as a fellow communist? After all, it was not Marx who established the final criterion for judging the authenticity of one's life as a concern for all peoples in need. It was comrade Jesus. How do we move beyond a New Left narrative of redistribution and defence of public services? How do we get up and running an antagonistic social and political paradigm to neoliberalism? How can forms of popular power from below be transferred into a new historical bloc? How do we recompose ourselves into an anti-capitalist united front? We need leadership from below that can help us build political programs, articulate new non-commodified collective practices, including new forms of self-management and new forms of public ownership and networks of redistribution—in short, a credible alternative to capitalism that begins with an engagement in the struggles of and for our times. These are the questions that need to be exercised by critical educators everywhere. For these are the questions asked of us by the future of history.

References

Adorno, T. (1962). *Prisms*. MIT Press.

Amin, S. (2010, February 7). *The battlefields chosen by contemporary imperialism: Conditions for an effective response from the South*. MRZine. http://mrzine.monthlyreview.org/2010/amin070210.html

Anderson, K. (2010, August 18). *Overcoming some current challenges to dialectical thought*. International Marxist-Humanist. http://www.internationalmarxisthumanist.org/articles/overcoming-some-current-challenges-to-dialectical-thought

Blum, W. (2014a, August 11). Cold War 2. *Anti-empire report, #131*. http://williamblum.org/aer/read/131

*Brandon, S.G.F. (1967). *Jesus and the zealots*. Charles Scribner's Sons.

Clark, J.P. (2013). *The impossible community: Realizing communitarian anarchism* (see pp. 217–245). Bloomsbury.

Dunayevskaya, R. (1992). *The Marxist-humanist theory of state capitalism*. The News & Letters Committee (Chicago).

Ebert, T. (2009). *The task of cultural critique*. University of Illinois Press.

Ebert, T., & Zavarzadeh, M. (2007). *Class in culture.* Paradigm.
Fatheuer, T. (2011). *Buen vivir: A brief introduction to Latin America's new concepts for the good life and the rights of nature.* Heinrich Böll Foundation Publication Series on Ecology, vol. 17. Heinrich Böll Foundation.
Fischman, G.E., & McLaren, P. (2005). Rethinking critical pedagogy and the Gramscian and Freirean legacies: From organic to committed intellectuals or critical pedagogy, commitment, and praxis. *Cultural Studies <=> Critical Methodologies,* 5(4), 425–446. https://amadlandawonye.wikispaces.com/2005,+McLaren+and+Fischman,+Gramsci,+Freire,+Organic+Intellectuals
Hudis, P. (2005, November). *Marx's critical appropriation and transcendence of Hegel's theory of alienation.* Presentation to Brecht Forum, New York City.
Hudis, P. (2012). *Marx's concept of the alternative to capitalism.* Haymarket Books. http://dx.doi.org/10.1163/9789004229860
McLaren, P. (2014a). Contemporary youth resistance culture and the class struggle. *Critical Arts,* 28(1), 152–160. http://dx.doi.org/10.1080/02560046.2014.883701
Miranda, J.P. (1977). *Being and the Messiah: The message of St. John.* Orbis Books.
Miranda, J.P. (2004). *Communism in the Bible,* trans. Robert R. Barr. Wipf & Stock.
Pomeroy, A.F. (2004). Why Marx, why now? A recollection of Dunayevskaya's *Power of negativity. Cultural Logic,* 7. http://clogic.eserver.org/2004/pomeroy.html
Reitz, C. (2000). *Art, alienation and the humanities: A critical engagement with Herbert Marcuse.* SUNY Press.
Reitz, C. (2013). Conclusion: the Commonwealth counter-offensive. In C. Reitz (Ed.), *Crisis and commonwealth: Marcuse, Marx, McLaren,* pp. 269–286. Lexington Books.
Rivage-Seul, M. (2014, April 27). (Sunday homily) *Christianity is communism! Jesus was a communist!* OpEdNews. http://www.opednews.com/articles/Sunday-Homily-Christiani-by-Mike-Rivage-Seul-Christianity_Communism_Economic_Jesus-140426-205.html
San Juan, E. (2007). *In the wake of terror: Class, race, nation, ethnicity in the postmodern world.* Lexington Books.
Sethness, J. (2013, June 16). *The structural violence that is capitalism.* Truthout. http://www.truth-out.org/opinion/item/16887-the-structural-genocide-that-is-capitalism
Torrance, R.M. (1994). *The spiritual quest: Transcendence in myth, religion, and science.* University of California Press.

Endnote

1 This chapter was presented at Chapman University in 2014. What appears here is an abridged version of that speech.

CHAPTER EIGHT

Postdigital Gathering

PETAR JANDRIĆ

Introduction

THIS COLLECTION OF LETTERS responds to Peter McLaren's 2014 article, "Comrade Jesus. The Dialectic Regained: An Epistolic Manifesto." Starting from dialogues between Peter McLaren and Petar Jandrić during a decade of working together, it develops a more general concept of postdigital gathering. The chapter examines various transformations of today's critical pedagogy in our postdigital condition, with an emphasis on dialectics, the concept of the public intellectual, and epistemology. It launches a critique of the contemporary critical pedagogy movement and elaborates on the need to develop critical pedagogy toward human-technology relationships and critical posthumanism. Emphasizing the importance of myth and faith in human affairs, the chapter calls for a reinvention of traditional critical pedagogy through new forms of postdigital gathering.

Dear Peter,

After a decade of daily correspondence, after more than thirty co-authored articles and a book, after numerous visits to your various homes (the flat above the gun shop in Orange was really something ☺), and after becoming close friends and soulmates, I was asked to publicly dialogue your text and apply it to my own context, practice, research, or philosophy. I regularly engage with works of other scholars—after all, such public dialogues are bread and butter of academic knowledge production. In your case, however, this innocent call has left me in awe—what else can I say about your work, that we have not covered, or will not cover, in our writings together?

As I read your email of today, I see you sitting in your living room, I smell something nice from your kitchen, I hear Angie quietly flipping pages of her book on the sofa. When you mention talking to Suzi or Charlotte or Kevin, I see their faces and hear their laughter. When you say that you just returned from Chapman University's campus, I see that schizophrenic mesh-up of statues representing people from Paulo Freire to Ayn Rand, and beautiful students lounging by the lush centrepiece swimming pool, in bright Californian sun. I see you, I smell you, I feel you. I usually cannot touch you, unless we're together in Greece, Croatia, California, Canada, Turkey, and various other places where we've met over the years. But you are in my pocket all the time, lurking from my phone's screen, often much closer to my heart than my next-door neighbour. I know, without asking, that you feel the same.

Our age difference spans 30 years of the quickest technological development in human history, and our spatial distance is 15+ hours on an aeroplane. Your background is in Shakespeare, and mine is in quantum mechanics. You live in advanced capitalism of the U.S., and I live in a post-communist country with free healthcare and education. But during the past ten years that we have grown together, these differences never presented a problem; they only fertilized our growth. Your context has become my context, and my context has become your context. Your practice has become my practice, and my practice has become your practice. Your research has become my research, and my research has become your research. Your philosophy has become my philosophy, and my philosophy has become your philosophy.

However, being together does not imply being the same or idolizing the other (Jandrić, 2019). It would be easy to pick one or another point of our disagreement and offer counter-arguments. Being an atheist, I could challenge human need for religious belief. Being an anarchist and living in East Europe, I could say a lot against your stubborn calls for socialism. Brought up in Christian faith, I could challenge the idea that Jesus was the first Marxist. But we discussed these and many other issues in our numerous writings together, and I don't want to repeat old discussions. So I will just follow my free associations, and comment on a selection of themes from your article in no particular order—just like we do in our daily email exchanges.

Dear Peter

Do you remember our first meeting at a conference in Athens, Greece, in 2011? We ate, drank, protested, ran away from the police, and were tear-gassed (or did tear-gas happen in Ankara a bit later?). Our first interview has inspired the development of the book in which I interviewed more than 20 interlocutors from all over the world. *Learning in the Age of Digital Reason* (Jandrić, 2017) was my first attempt at creating a global online dialogue, and this line of research culminated in our latest book, *Postdigital Dialogues* (McLaren & Jandrić, 2020).

During this decade I began theorizing our postdigital condition, which is a curious blend between our online and offline existence, and which is "hard to define; messy; unpredictable; digital and analog; technological and non-technological; biological and informational" (Jandrić et al., 2018, p. 895). I started connecting people with similar interests, and created two online gathering spaces—*Postdigital Science and Education* journal[1] and book series[2]—that you are a founding member. Amongst numerous themes of interest, you, I, and many others, explored postdigital dialogue and concluded that it may generate "genuine, substantive, radical or participatory democracy, focusing on the interactive over the institutional, thus committing and contributing to political struggles in, against and beyond capitalism" (Jandrić et al., 2019, p. 180). There is no way that I can distinguish this scholarly work from my personal life—our postdigital gathering simply does not see such borders.

Having said that, your (work on) dialectics arrives from a different perspective. For you, Peter, "[t]he revolution is now, it's the dialectic regained, it's the people unchained, it's the eschaton made immanent." You are focused on developing a collective understanding that we exist in the world with others, through your interpretation of Hegel's negation of the negation, which "establishes a relation with itself, freeing itself from the external object it is attempting to negate," and which is required to free us from the chains of capitalism. Your dialectic, Peter, allows us to imagine radically different futures while keeping good parts of our past.

This is an important place of gathering between "my" postdigital theory and "your" dialectic. "The postdigital is both a rupture in our existing theories and their continuation" (Jandrić et al., 2018, p. 895). Indeed, Peter, I see your dialectic as a crucial rupture and continuation of theories and (perhaps more importantly) social relationships in and for our postdigital times. As we concluded together in *Postdigital Dialogues* (McLaren & Jandrić, 2020), postdigital critical praxis must be dialectical. So how do we develop this postdigital dialectic from a theoretical academic exercise into a transformative social force?

Dear Peter

Our postdigital dialogue, or postdigital gathering—and when I say "our," I don't mean our little duo but the whole world of like-minded people—is generative at so many levels. Since its foundation in 2018, *Postdigital Science and Education* has published almost 200 scholarly articles and several books which display potentials of postdigital gathering in theory, policy, and practice. *Postdigital Science and Education* is just one of many scholarly examples, but the world is full of people who think, act, and live critical pedagogy without any academic underpinnings. So how do we bring all these people together and make a real change?

It has become increasingly obvious that our postdigital gathering, deeply intertwined with but not restricted to the Internet, also requires new forms of individual and social engagement. I will not succumb to the temptation of reproducing some of our writings about postdigital critical public intellectuals, which illuminate how we might develop our praxis towards the future, except for saying that "the tradition of critical pedagogy provides indispensable theoretical background for contemporary intellectuals, yet our strategies and practices are in a need for constant reconceptualization in and for postdigital times we live in" (Jandrić & McLaren, 2020).

A few years ago, in an interview for *Learning in the Age of Digital Reason*, Fred Turner spoke a line that has remained with me forever: "Network intellectuals I think are simultaneously masters of ideas and masters of social worlds. In fact, it is the mastery of the social world that leads to the ideas. Not vice versa" (in Jandrić, 2017, p. 71). Building on this thought, Derek Ford and I recently wrote:

> Networks have replaced the detached academic, who if they are to join in the new pedagogy of the public intellectual will do so not as an academic but as a node in an ever-expanding network. It is with this message that we welcome the birth of the postdigital public intellectual into our world who, it should be clear by now, is always already a collective assemblage whose educational logics run along the lines of collective postdigital study, and not traditional teaching and learning. (Ford & Jandrić, 2019, p. 105)

The postdigital mesh-up between our biological and technological existence, implied but often hidden in all those apps and services which measure our heartbeats and steps developed by your neoliberal neighbours in Silicon Valley, implies the need to build new postdigital collective assemblages. So how should we go about that task?

Dear Peter

You very well know that Paulo Freire was a big proponent of computers and other technologies, yet our contemporaries who consider themselves as Freire's most faithful followers seem to have forgotten that message (Kahn & Kellner, 2007). I can sympathise with this resistance towards digitalization (Malott, 2020), especially when looking at the Californian ideology which dominates Silicon Valley policy and practice (Barbrook & Cameron, 1996). According to this dominant narrative, numerous human activities from transport (e.g., Uber) through accommodation (e.g., Airbnb), to education (e.g., Massive Open Online Courses, or MOOCs), are ripe for disruption (Jandrić & Hayes, 2020). While it is easy to agree that human activities can and should be improved, the Silicon Valley idea of disruption is always the same: automate operations, lay off workers, and put profit into the hands of a small circle of technology owners (Williamson, 2019; Arantes, 2020). In this view, technical development becomes neoliberal capitalism on steroids.

Thankfully, the Californian ideology is not the only game in town, and there are other, more humanistic approaches which open up spaces for true critical pedagogy. At this point I will not write about practical examples, such as platform cooperativism, which can be found in my other works (e.g., Jandrić and Hayes, 2019). Instead, I will delve deeper and start with the French philosopher Pierre Lévy's broad definition of collective intelligence as

> a scientific, technical and political project that aims to make people smarter with computers, instead of trying to make computers smarter than people. So, collective intelligence is neither the opposite of collective stupidity nor the opposite of individual intelligence. It is the opposite of artificial intelligence. It is a way to grow a renewed human/cultural cognitive system by exploiting our increasing computing power and our ubiquitous memory. (Peters, 2015, p. 261)

Applying these theories to education, critical post-humanists such as Siân Bayne explore the spaces "where the social and the material worlds come together—where the human teacher's agency comes up against the workings of data to conduct another, and different, kind of teaching which is neither human nor mechanic but some kind of gathering of the two" (in Jandrić, 2017, p. 206). I won't lament further about one of my favourite fields, philosophy of technology, but I do need to say that contemporary critical pedagogy would do itself a big favour by following in the footsteps of the Frankfurt School of Social Science and getting a firmer grip on human-technology relationships, especially as they relate to the question of what it means to be human in our postdigital age (see Fawns, 2019). Before we embark on this journey, however, we need to ask (see Knox, 2019): What does this entail in relation to knowledge?

Dear Peter

In "Comrade Jesus" you call for an epistemological alternative inspired by Fatheuer's (2011) ideas about the right to a "good life" (*buen vivir*), the concept of Mother Earth (*Pachamama*), and Christian mystics, amongst other influences. Your epistemological alternative aims to "to help stave off the epistemicide of indigenous knowledges by means of violent Eurocentric practices," and to develop "a class struggle of transnational reach." We already agreed elsewhere, Peter, that this new epistemology cannot be thought of without addressing postdigital challenges (McLaren & Jandrić, 2020). (It is worthwhile to mention that "Comrade Jesus" was written before our many discussions about our postdigital reality.) As I wrote recently (inspired by Peters & Besley, 2019), understanding of individual human experience, huge amounts of data produced by this human experience, and power relationships which co-produce the human experience—as they relate to traditional themes of critical pedagogy such as social justice and education—bring about the need for a new critical philosophy of the postdigital (Jandrić, 2021).

This is where I need to launch a hugely uncomfortable but equally necessary critique of today's critical pedagogy movement—a critique I believe we agree upon in general terms, but which may also spark some disagreement. Trapped in endless classroom and community space reinventions of Freire's *circulo de la cultura*, balkanized into various cliques and communities claiming that their critical pedagogy is better than that of their next-door neighbours, informally led by people who claim this or that sort of ownership over critical pedagogy based on their past and/or present achievements, too many critical pedagogues of today carry, as Raoul Vaneigem once said, "a corpse in their mouth" (1975) [1967]; we developed this argument in detail in Jandrić & McLaren, 2020. Unfortunately, however, today's critical pedagogy movement largely ignores "blurred and messy relationships between physics and biology, old and new media, humanism and posthumanism, knowledge capitalism and bio-informational capitalism" (Jandrić et al., 2018, p. 896) characteristic of our postdigital age. This critique is related to numerous factors such as politics and economy of today's academic work, yet deep inside, its essence is epistemological.

Unsurprisingly, the latest generation of critical pedagogy recognizes these problems very well. In the words of Derek Ford, "critical pedagogy is at a deadend. This is not to say that it offers nothing valuable, but rather that it has been stagnant for some time (I would say at least since the beginning of the 21st century)" (Ford, 2017, p. 2). It is not a surprise that people born into the world of computers understand the need to reinvent Freire in and for our postdigital age, yet you, Peter, are amongst a few early architects of the first wave of North American critical pedagogy who do not shy away from these topics. We need more people who are able to connect traditional critical pedagogy and our postdigital condition—and we need them urgently. Here, abovementioned epistemological questions translate into more practical questions pertaining to research methodology. As we emphasized in our works (Jandrić, 2016; McLaren & Jandrić, 2020), answers to these questions lie in accepting one or another form of transcending disciplinary borders such as trans- and post-disciplinarity. And this conclusion begs another important question: How do we connect all those things together?

Dear Peter

Your response to this question, in "Comrade Jesus" and also elsewhere (McLaren, 2019, 2020), reaches beyond scholarly inquiry and into the realm of myth and faith. Coming from an ex-communist country which has quickly reformed into one of Europe's bastions of fundamentalist Catholicism, it took me a while to fathom the value of your claim—a detailed description of my intellectual journey can be found in my concluding thoughts in *Postdigital Dialogues*, and which culminated in the following statement:

> By now, however, postdigital theory has largely failed to grasp that humans are not only beings of logic and emotion—we are also beings of myth and faith . . . . We want what others want, we seek purification through ritual sacrifice, we are prone to various archetypes, we are puzzled by duality between mind and matter, and we ask, in Peter's words, "if humans developed as a random occurrence or whether we are here for a reason." We seek the eschaton of freedom and justice, although we know that we will never get there. We know that people and machines need to work together, but we cannot agree how—even when it comes to our own survival as a species. So how do we even try to reach beyond the academic ivory tower and seek real change? (McLaren & Jandrić, 2020, p. 255)

I don't know the answer to this question, and neither do you. As you repeated many times, often using beautiful words written by the poet Antonio Machado, we make the road by walking (*Caminante, no hay camino, se hace camino al andar*).

We need to walk this walk together, and we need to walk it now. Yesterday could have been better, tomorrow may be too late. While you, I, Suzi, Charlotte, Kevin, and many other friends and comrades understand this need, our community urgently needs to expand and create a strong critical front aimed against the evils of today and toward development of a better society. We need to conscientise others about traditional insights of critical pedagogy, and we need to reinvent critical pedagogy in and for our postdigital age. Our gathering over the last decade shows that it is possible to be together, and appreciate all differences between us, in the uncanny space between the physical and the digital that we now call the postdigital (Jandrić & Kuzmanić, 2020). We are walking a frightening path, but we have each other and our shared (religious and non-religious) faith that a better world is possible.

Yours,
Petar

References

Arantes, J.A. (2020). The servitization of Australian K–12 educational settings. *Postdigital Science and Education*, 491–515.

Barbrook, R., & Cameron, A. (1996). The Californian ideology. *Science as Culture*, 6(1), 44–72.

Fatheuer, T. (2011) *Buen vivir: A brief introduction to Latin America's new concepts for the good life and the rights of nature.* Heinrich Böll Foundation Publication Series on Ecology, vol. 17. Heinrich Böll Foundation.

Fawns, T. (2019). Postdigital education in design and practice. *Postdigital Science and Education*, 1(1), 132–145.

Ford, D.R. (2017). *Education and the production of space: Political pedagogy, geography, and urban revolution.* Routledge.

Ford, D.R., & Jandrić, P. (2019). The public intellectual is dead, long live the public intellectual! The postdigital rebirth of public pedagogy. *Critical Questions in Education*, 10(2), 92–106.

Freire, P. (1972). *Pedagogy of the oppressed.* Penguin Education Specials.

Jandrić, P. (2016). The methodological challenge of networked learning: (Post)disciplinarity and critical emancipation. In T. Ryberg, C. Sinclair, S. Bayne, & de M. Laat (Eds.), *Research, boundaries, and policy in networked learning*, pp. 165–181. Springer.

Jandrić, P. (2017). *Learning in the age of digital reason.* Sense.

Jandrić, P. (2019). We-think, we-learn, we-act: The trialectic of postdigital collective intelligence. *Postdigital Science and Education*, 1(2), 257–279.

Jandrić, P. (2021). The postdigital challenge of critical educational research. In C. Mathias (Ed.), *Critical theoretical research methods in education.* Routledge.

Jandrić, P., & Hayes, S. (2019). The postdigital challenge of redefining education from the margins. *Learning, Media and Technology*, 44(3), 381–393.

Jandrić, P., & Hayes, S. (2020). Postdigital we-learn. *Studies in Philosophy of Education*, 39(3), 285–297.

Jandrić, P., & Kuzmanić, A. (2020). Uncanny. *Postdigital Science and Education*, 2(2), 239–244.

Jandrić, P., & McLaren, P. (2020). Postdigital cross border reflections on critical utopia. *Educational Philosophy and Theory*, 52(14), 1–13.

Jandrić, P., Knox, J., Besley, T., Ryberg, T., Suoranta, J., & Hayes, S. (2018). Postdigital science and education. *Educational Philosophy and Theory*, 50(10), 893–899.

Jandrić, P., Ryberg, T., Knox, J., Lacković, N., Hayes, S., Suoranta, J., Smith, M., Steketee, A., Peters, M.A., McLaren, P., Ford, D.R., Asher, G., McGregor, C., Stewart, G., Williamson, B., & Gibbons, A. (2019). Postdigital dialogue. *Postdigital Science and Education*, 1(1), 163–189.

Kahn, R., & Kellner, D. (2007). Paulo Freire and Ivan Illich: Technology, politics and the reconstruction of education. *Policy Futures in Education*, 5(4), 431–448.

Knox, J. (2019). What does the "postdigital" mean for education? Three critical perspectives on the digital, with implications for educational research and practice. *Postdigital Science and Education*, 2(1), 357–370.

Malott, C. (2020). The sublation of digital education. *Postdigital Science and Education*, 2(2), 365–379.
McLaren, P. (2014). Comrade Jesus. The dialectic regained: An epistolic manifesto. *Knowledge Cultures*, 2(6), 55–114.
McLaren, P. (2019). Reclaiming the present or a return to the ash heap of the future? *Postdigital Science and Education*, 1(1), 10–13.
McLaren, P. (2020). Networked religion: Metaphysical redemption or eternal regret? *Postdigital Science and Education*, 3, 294–306.
McLaren, P., & Jandrić, P. (2020). *Postdigital dialogues on critical pedagogy, liberation theology and information technology*. Bloomsbury.
Peters, M.A. (2015). Interview with Pierre A. Lévy, French philosopher of collective intelligence. *Open Review of Educational Research*, 2(1), 259–266.
Peters, M.A., & Besley, T. (2019). Critical philosophy of the postdigital. *Postdigital Science and Education*, 1(1), 29–42.
Vaneigem, R. (1975 [1967]). *The revolution of everyday life*. Practical Paradise.
Williamson, B. (2019). Brain data: Scanning, scraping and sculpting the plastic learning brain through neurotechnology. *Postdigital Science and Education*, 1(1), 65–86.

Endnotes

1 https://www.springer.com/journal/42438.
2 https://www.springer.com/series/16439.

CHAPTER NINE

In Conversation with Peter:

Becoming Teachers and Scholars for Social Change

Charlotte Achieng-Evensen and Kevin Stockbridge

In his opening statement in Chapter Seven herein, "Comrade Jesus, the Dialectic Regained: An Epistolic Manifesto," Peter McLaren (hereafter cited as McLaren, Chapter Seven herein) contends that corporations strive to convince us that public schools are broken. Consequently, our capitalist culture venerates private ownership as the only solution to the *brokenness* of schools. Essentially, corporations endeavor to position themselves as best suited to educating students for democratic citizenship. For Peter, this act of corporate privatization in schools is a feat of social engineering contrived to turn citizens into automatons in bed with the "logic of capitalist accumulation and profit" (McLaren, Chapter Seven herein). Such treatment of humans-as-products in service of the cost-analyzed bottom line is aided by peddling "critical thinking" as an incentivized tool "to create a privatized discount store version of democracy allied with the arrogance and greed of the ruling class" (McLaren, Chapter Seven herein). Peter enters this conversation by adopting the language of Marxist humanism, revolutionary critical pedagogy, and Christian socialism. His words inspire our imaginations in pursuit of liberatory practice.

As Peter's former students, we respond to his chapter by engaging in dialogue. We approach the conversation as contextual, as human realities representing moments of shared experience. In general, conversation, personal meanings, questions, and hopes intermingle. That fusion occurs here as we bring an exploration of our own experiences, positionality, and meaning-making to the text. We are reminded of a question Dr. Suzanne SooHoo would ask: "Where are *you* in this work?" In response, we interrogate elements of our identities, epistemologies, and pedagogies as they commingle with Peter's words.

On Identity

Peter's writing demonstrates not only his intellectual commitment to the work of liberation, but his vulnerable self-revelation as a fellow sojourner on the path to humanization. He notes: "We find our praxis of universal solidarity in suffering and hope and in our collective recognition that we are not alone but exist in the world with others" (McLaren, Chapter Seven herein). Our solidarity with Peter is felt in our shared yearning for the more just and equitable world of which he speaks. As companions in this historical act of *becoming*, we pause to be vulnerable, like Peter, by naming who we are and from where we enter into this shared space of dialogue (Freire, 1970).

Charlotte: I enter this conversation from the vantage point of a decolonial scholar learning the cadences and lineages of her field, as well as a seasoned K–12 practitioner. My purpose is to trouble the same sullied waters that Peter troubles. I seek, like him, the practice of purchasing "a crisper more perspicuous reality" (McLaren, Chapter Seven herein). And, I wonder, what does clarity actually entail? As we lean into this goal of reconceptualizing and reconstructing notions of schooling, I reflect on two questions: Who participates in defining the goal(s) for transformation? Who decides its often volatile and necessary dynamic modes? There is a Swahili proverb stating umoja ni nguvu (*Swahili Proverbs*, 2021). Loosely translated, these words invite us to consider unity as strength. Of course, unity does not mean sameness. Tuck and Yang (2012), in their lucid discussion regarding the aims of decolonization, remind us that "solidarity is an uneasy, reserved, and unsettled matter that neither reconciles present grievances nor forecloses future conflict" (p. 3). For Tuck and Yang (2012), our discourses and our actions must account for the subtle and explicit ways in which oppressive systems, particularly settler colonialism, engulf the work of justice. We must remain "*unsettled.*" Can "radical reconstruction" occur without the rituals of coming together—even and specifically to be against, to reconstitute? If indeed the goal of education is a radical reconstruction of society, then the togetherness of shaping our terms of engagement must necessarily be different. But, different how? Peter, inspired by Fatheuer (2011), imagines that "it is important to point out that *buen vivir* is not a return to ancestral, traditional thinking, but is a type of *chi'ixi*, or a concept where something can exist and not exist at the same time . . ." (McLaren, Chapter Seven herein). I ask, is it possible to exist with contradictions?

Kevin: I might define myself, at best, as a *budding scholar*. I am only a few years beyond the defense of my doctoral dissertation. Since that time, critical pedagogy and queer theory have predominated my academic musings on education. As a queer man, I am skeptical of socially constructed binaries, believing that these defined exclusionary boundaries of difference are the structural supports that enable oppression (Jagose, 1996; Sedgwick, 1990; Kumashiro, 2002). I often wonder what new world might be revealed beyond these binaries. Such a world could only take shape in spaces of radical solidarity (SooHoo et al., 2018). It is for this reason that "critical revolutionary pedagogy is non-sectarian and emphasizes ecumenical approaches" (McLaren, Chapter Seven herein). I read the problems and possibilities of public education along with Peter through this lens.

I also approach this conversation as a *teacher educator*. In this position, I look with great sadness at public education and the trajectory that it intends to set for our society. I commiserate with Peter (McLaren, Chapter Seven herein) as he decries "not only [official education's] puerile understanding of the meaning and purpose of public knowledge, but its hypocrisy in advocating critical thinking." Predominant educational practices have produced post-secondary students who conceive of teaching and learning as functionalist realities. Engaging in teacher education for a more just future means revealing the ideological momentum of uncritical concepts of education and the hegemonic discourses they perpetuate (Apple, 1979). Breaking the cycle of determinist ideas in education is absolutely necessary if we hope to build a future that begins to reflect the concept of *buen vivir* to which Peter refers.

On Epistemology

Under the threat of erasure by current regimes of educational corporatization, we find myriad ways of knowing providing us pathways for imagining a future in which humanity and nature might thrive. The incongruence of these epistemologies to capitalistic aims makes them a menace to the status quo.

Henry Giroux (2016) notes that in today's "pedagogy of repression, students are conditioned to unlearn any respect for democracy, justice, and what it might mean to connect learning to social change" (p. 355). In this educational milieu, Peter reminds us that "a larger epistemological fight against neoliberal and imperial common sense" (p. 22) must be waged.

Kevin: Peter's words invite me to peer at the world through the lens of his critical and well-informed mind. Coming to know and understand reality in this way requires the disciplined use of interpenetrating aspects of our humanity: imagination, reason, morality, spirituality, community, action, and curiosity. Such knowledge transgresses the constructivist/objectivist binary of epistemology. This dualism only permits either an epistemology of detachment or one of determinism. Caught in the snares of these theories, we find ourselves desperately seeking a cause for hope (Freire, 1994). We must come to know in a way that "recognizes consciousness and external reality as mutually constitutive, and asserts that there must be an ethical dimension that gives priority to the oppressed" (McLaren, Chapter Seven herein). Knowing in this way is dynamic, inspiring constant social activity relative to a moral mandate for humanization, and is thereby subject to ethical accountability.

How do we shift goodness from being the object of knowledge to becoming the purpose and direction of knowing? This is the ethical, epistemological revolution of critical pedagogy. It reconstitutes the telos of knowing as "the return of humanity to itself" (McLaren, Chapter Seven herein). As Peter insists, this is not simply the return of the *idea* of humanity to its origins. It means a full reconciliation of self, community, and place in all their dignity. In order to do this, we must have a more expansive understanding of knowing, one that serves this humanizing mission. I am reminded of Myers's (2013) elucidation of a holographic epistemology with its grounding in indigenous ways of knowing. She notes the need for embracing knowledge that is physical, mental, and spiritual. A fully human knowledge requires that one "*see* the science in it, *think* it through carefully, and then *inspire* the world with the quality of your participation" (Myers, 2013, p. 100). If I want such knowledge to take root in the lives of my students, I must question whether my pedagogical practices promote this kind of fullness.

Charlotte: As a racialized individual who is simultaneously a K–12 practitioner, the felt pressure of extinction is both relentless and ever-present. It is sneaky, alienating the individual into self-defined practices of covert autonomy.

Moment by moment, I am consistently engaging the rituals of place-making. I am acutely aware that the system in which I work intentionally seeks to erase my histories and ways of knowing, relegating these into ahistorical, inferior aberrations on the way to superiority in human achievement. Without the depth of self-reflection as to how such deep macrostructures work to reinforce the oppression of dehumanization, I can become siloed in my pushback against the system, I can become shackled by the boundaries created by the system. I have to constantly remind myself that these structures are intentionally created to colonize. Therefore, the opportunities for enacting transformation and just social change can become a life-sucking, relentless struggle against the dominant structure. Schooling reproduces neoliberal capitalist structures in greater society.

Peter argues that we find ourselves subject to circumstances "created by social relations of production and the way in which neo-liberal capitalism has produced nature/human relations as a total world ecology linked to a racialized social division of labor and hyper-nationalism" (McLaren, Chapter Seven herein). For me, these words affirm the experiential resistance I encounter within school settings.

On Pedagogy

Peter's repudiation of a soulless and uncritical education is strongly felt in his chapter. Public education is predominated by "necrophilic" pedagogies that promote "a mechanistic, static, naturalistic, spatialized view of consciousness" (Freire, 1970). Yet, not all hope is lost! Peter reminds us that "Critical pedagogy offers an alternative vision and set of goals for the education of humanity" (Chapter Seven herein). As critical educators, we cannot help but examine our practices in conversation with his words.

Charlotte: In thinking about pedagogy, I am reminded that the classroom is a place of mutuality and, therefore, hope. I do not teach alone; neither am I alone in the processes of learning. Pedagogy, the ways in which teaching and learning is carried out within learning spaces, is transformed by my ability to engage with students in deeply humanizing ways. Kessi, Marks, and Ramugondo (2020) remind us that "structures, epistemologies and actions alike are dependent on human relations; we sustain and replicate systems of power and exclusion" (p. 275). I am deeply aware that when I am not intentional about my movement, my being as a teacher, then I am prone to replicating oppressive institutional dynamics. I am constantly seeking, as Peter articulates, to "know [my]herself as a source of the movement of the real … as agents of self-determination, hear themselves speak, and are able both to denounce oppression and the evils of the world and to announce, in Freire's terms, a liberating alternative" (McLaren, Chapter Seven herein). It is this knowledge and this engagement with and apart from self that allows me to hope along with students. Collectively, we seek transformation.

Kevin: Peter references the current state of affairs by noting that public education is geared toward an exclusive and privatized democracy. Given the deepening of social fissures that continue to reveal the fallacy of a truly united country, we are all the more desperate for pedagogy aligned with our greatest hopes for a just and unified society. The fact that many of my graduate students seem to struggle with expressing their voice in the classroom is a product of a "banking" education (Freire, 1970). Pedagogies that prioritize content over pupil are at odds with the development of agentic citizens. A change is desperately needed. "This occurs when human beings, as agents of self-determination, hear themselves speak, and are able both to denounce oppression and the evils of the world and to announce, in Freire's terms, a liberating alternative" (McLaren, Chapter Seven herein). I wonder what might happen to our democracy if solidarity and togetherness were at the center of our curricula (Hogg et al., 2021).

When I ask students to co-create and ratify classroom norms with me at the beginning of each semester, they are unsure of how to deal with the shared power of a democratic space. This is always an uncomfortable activity for them, and at least one student requests that I take all power over making classroom decisions. My students are experts at reproducing performances of compliance when they start the semester. My hope is to disrupt this compliant expertise through a new kind of learning. And, as Kumashiro (2004) insists, "Learning is a disorienting process that raises questions about what was already learned and what has yet to be learned" (p. 30). To foil the replication of unjust social norms, Peter notes, demands "a deliberate and urgent effort by teachers and teacher educators to transcend, through self-transformation, the limits of everyday reality and the human condition under capitalism" (p. 21). Thus, I need to interrogate my own teacher identity and the aims of my practice by engaging in pedagogy with my students that is co-directed, co-assessed, and communal. This is all the more important when this process is discomforting for me. Only by doing this can my classroom be a place in which a more just and robust democracy prefiguratively takes shape in the present (Bolin, 2017; Zavala & Golden, 2016).

A Conversational Pause . . .

We began this textual dialogue by considering Peter's deliberation on the state of public schools. We pause here, reflecting on his conceptions of a liberating alternative, a reconstruction of schools as democratic, transformative spaces. Our conversation carries on, expanding out of these pages and into our teaching practice, our ideological reasoning, and our formation as educators. Certainly, we continue pondering his call to transcend beyond our current structures, to imagine beyond our current ways of knowing. In Peter's words, "The revolution is now, it's the dialectic regained, it's the people unchained, it's the eschaton made immanent" (McLaren, Chapter Seven herein).

References

Apple, M. (1979). *Ideology and curriculum.* Routledge.

Bolin, T.D. (2017). Struggling for democracy: Paulo Freire and transforming society through education. *Policy Futures in Education*, 15(6), 744–766. https://doi.org/10.1177/1478210317721311

Fatheuer, T. (2011) *Buen vivir: A brief introduction to Latin America's new concepts for the good life and the rights of nature.* Heinrich Böll Foundation Publication Series on Ecology, vol. 17. Heinrich Böll Foundation.

Freire, P. (1970). *Pedagogy of the oppressed.* Continuum.

Freire, P. (1994). *Pedagogy of hope.* Continuum.

Giroux, H. (2016). When schools become dead zones of the imagination: A critical pedagogy manifesto. *The High School Journal*, 99(4), 351–359.

Hogg, L., Stockbridge, K., Achieng-Evensen, C., & SooHoo, S. (Eds.). (2021). *Pedagogies of with-ness: Students, teachers, voice, and agency.* Myers Education Press.

Jagose, A. (1996). *Queer theory: An introduction.* NYU Press.

Kessi, S., Marks, Z., & Ramugondo, E. (2020). Decolonizing African studies. *Critical African Studies*, 12(3), 271–282. https://doi.org/https://doi.org/10.1080/21681392.2020.181341

Kumashiro, K. (2002). *Troubling education: Queer activism and anti-oppressive pedagogy.* Routledge.

Kumashiro, K. (2004). *Against common sense: Teaching and learning toward social justice.* Routledge.

McLaren, A. (2021). Comrade Jesus, the dialectic regained: An epistolic manifesto (Chapter Seven in the present volume). Myers Education Press.

Myers, M.A. (2013). Holographic epistemology: Native common sense. *China Media Research*, 9(2), 94–101.

Sedgwick, E.K. (1990). *Epistemology of the closet.* University of California Press.
SooHoo, S., Huerta, P., Huerta-Meza, P., Bolin, T., & Stockbridge, K. (2018). *Let's chat—Cultivating community university dialogue: A coffee table textbook on partnerships.* Myers Education Press.
Swahili proverbs: Methali za Kiswahili. (2021). http://swahiliproverbs.afrst.illinois.edu/proverbssecond.htm
Tuck, E., & Yang, K.W. (2012). Decolonization is not a metaphor. *Decolonization: Indigeneity, Education & Society*, 1(1), 1–40.
Zavala, M., & Golden, N.A. (2016). Prefiguring alternative worlds: Organic critical literacies and socio-cultural revolutions. *Knowledge Cultures*, 4(6), 207–227.

Section Three: Questions and Activity

Questions

1. Through the lens of public education as a construct, McLaren's introspective chapter broadly examines the question of justice and social transformation. As a reader, which elements of his chapter allow you to examine the social constructs of how our broader society is organized?
2. Crafted as a conversation, Achieng-Evensen and Stockbridge organize their chapter around themes of identity, epistemology, and pedagogy. Which deliberative frame(s) could you use to inform your understanding of self as a scholar-activist? Why?
3. Jandrić engages with McLaren in reflexive discourse pondering the reinvention of critical pedagogy for this current moment. How does his line of reasoning help you to clarify, expand, co-construct, and/or critique the concepts of post-digital dialogue and critical pedagogy?

Activity: Letter to Self

In Section 3, the authors engage in problem-posing through reflection and dialogue. Write a letter to yourself pondering your current context. How is who *you are* shaping, and being shaped by, your current personal, community, and work environments? How does engaging in this sort of reflection inform your action in the world?

Section Four

CHAPTER TEN

Freire and the Politics of Radical Consciousness[1]

ANTONIA DARDER

> *"It is sufficient to know that conscientization does not take place in abstract beings in the air but in real men and women and in social structures, to understand that it cannot remain on the level of the individual."*
>
> —Paulo Freire (1983)

FOR MORE THAN FOUR decades, Freire's writings have beckoned educators to embrace the struggle for critical consciousness and social transformation, with an uncompromising commitment to the most oppressed populations. It is, therefore, impossible for us to think about teaching critically and democratically in these difficult times, without understanding more deeply his concept of radical consciousness. Conscientização, or the process of critical awakening, belies any effort to objectify or abstract its very meaning. Instead, critical consciousness must always be understood as a road yet to be made; which, because it is unknown and unfinished, must be traced out step by step, in our organic relationships with the world and in the process of our labor as educators, activists, and revolutionary leaders.

The struggle for change begins, then, at that moment when human beings become both critically aware and fully intolerant of the oppressive conditions in which we find ourselves, and from there, transgress toward new ways of knowing and being in the world. This process signals moments of radical consciousness when individuals, in community, experience a breakthrough and decide to take another path, despite the crisis in education we are facing. Freire

(1998) considered the process of conscientização, or conscientization, as an essential principle of his pedagogy of love, in that it both opens the field for epistemological curiosity and ushers in radical possibilities for reinventing our world. Hence, consciousness, according to Paulo, "is one of the roads we have to follow if we are to deepen our awareness of the world, of facts, of events" (1998, p. 55). Freire's notion of human consciousness as unfinished also points to a critical evolutionary process whose openness can enliven our dialectical relationship with the world and beckons us toward emancipatory futures.

Freire, in dialogue with Myles Horton (Horton & Freire 1990), spoke adamantly of social consciousness as a dialectical process that develops and evolves, as we contend with the difficult social and educational conditions we find before us. Rather than adhere to prescribed roles and structures that oppress and repress our humanity, Paulo called for an emancipatory consciousness, through critical ways of teaching and living that require our ongoing participation together as cultural workers and historical subjects of the world. Committed to consciousness as a communal and democratic process, Freire (1998) asserted that "the breakthrough of a new form of awareness in understanding the world is not the privilege of one person. The experience that makes possible the 'breakthrough' is a collective experience" (77). This to say, we don't need the Lone Ranger or Superman to save us—instead we need one another if we are to genuinely live critically and democratically.

True to Paulo's understanding of knowledge as historical, there was a deepening in his articulation of the awakening of consciousness, or conscientização, over the years. This is particularly the case in his later writings, where he gave far greater salience to the role of feelings, sensations, and the body, in addition to the exercise of reason in the formation of consciousness. This is particularly evident in *Pedagogy of Freedom*, when Freire (1998) asserts that "What is important in teaching is not the mechanical repetition of this or that gesture but a comprehension of the value of sentiments, emotions, and desires . . . and sensibility, affectivity, and intuition" (p. 48). This powerful assertion of the value of our human faculties, beyond our reason, in the struggle for our liberation is a hallmark of Paulo Freire's pedagogy of love. His painstaking efforts to challenge the necrophilic grip of hegemonic schooling served to push forth a new integral rationality, infused with a communal understanding of a revolutionary consciousness as a living phenomenon of women and men in struggle.

Freire's concept of conscientização points to an understanding of critical awareness and the formation of radical consciousness as both a historical phenomenon and a human social process connected to our communal capacities to become authors and social actors of our destinies. However, Paulo emphasizes that critical consciousness neither occurs automatically, or naturally, nor should it be understood as an evolving linear phenomenon. Instead, he spoke to an emancipatory consciousness that arises through an organic process of human engagement, which requires human interactions that nurture our emancipatory relationship with the world. Only when we understand the dialectic relationship between consciousness and the world, "that is, when we know that we don't have a consciousness here and the world there; but, on the contrary, when both of them, the objectivity and the subjectivity, are incarnating dialectically, is it possible to understand what conscientização is, and to comprehend the role of consciousness in the liberation of humanity" (quoted in Davis, 1981, p. 62).

In writing about critical consciousness, Freire also anchors his conceptual meaning of conscientização based upon several key notions. First, he believed that the more accurately we come to grasp the true causality of our particular circumstances or conditions of life, the more critical our understanding of reality can be. Yet he provided an important caveat here: whatever is considered true today may not necessarily be true tomorrow. Freire posits here a historical and dialectical theory of meaning that must be understood both relationally and contextually. As history moves and conditions shift, so must our political readings of the world if we are to enable emancipatory life.

The second notion is an outcome of the first, in that critical awareness encompasses phenomena or facts, which exist empirically or experientially within particular circumstances that inform both a particular way of constructing knowledge and a mode of production. Therefore, through critical awareness of the world, as rooted in particular social and economic conditions of life, we can better comprehend our consciousness and the actions it informs as corresponding phenomena. Inherent in this revolutionary view of the world is the dialectical inseparability between consciousness and materiality.

And lastly, but similar to the latter, the nature of human actions and societal structures corresponds to the nature of prevailing epistemologies and ideologies, which, wittingly or unwittingly, inform the structures for communal life. Again, the world is not here and consciousness there. It is our consciousness that shapes the material world, as it is the material world that shapes our consciousness. Hence, if it is human beings who construct the world in which we live, then human beings are also capable, through changing our consciousness and social relationships, to transform our world. Herein is the foundation of Freire's concept of critical hope. Conscientização then entails the organic formation of an intimate relationship between consciousness, human action, and the world that we seek to transform and reinvent.

But most important, once again, Paulo emphasized the communal or social circumstances of solidarity that are required in its formation. Freire (1983) explained the deepening of consciousness in the following manner:[2]

> [It] is not and never can be an intellectual or an intellectualist effort. Conscientization cannot be arrived at by a psychological, idealist subjectivist road, nor through objectivism . . . . Just as the *prise de conscience* (or raising of consciousness) cannot operate in isolated individuals, but through the relations of transformation they establish between themselves and the world . . . [it] results . . . in a person's coming face to face with the world and with concrete reality . . . . This effort of [of consciousness] to transcend itself and achieve conscientization . . . always requires one's critical insertion in the reality which one begins to unveil, [and which] cannot be individual but social. (p. 148)

A powerful political dimension to the process of conscientização worth repeating is that critical consciousness, although it takes place in and emerges out of the expressed lived histories of each individual, cannot evolve and transform in the absence of others. More specifically, Paulo argued that "we cannot liberate the others, people cannot liberate themselves alone, because people liberate themselves in communion, mediated by [the] reality which they must transform" (Davis, 1981, p. 62). Also of note here is that Freire understood exceedingly well that the concept of consciousness could easily be distorted. In the first, it is through a sort of humanist idealism or liberal subjectivism that strips the concept of its criticality. Privileging individual subjectivity, it produces truths divorced from social context.

In the second, scientific objectivity reigns king, privileging so-called "objective" or "evidenced-based" truths, divorced from larger social and material conditions. In both instances, a false consciousness results (no matter how well meaning), narrowing the field of rationality, tyrannizing imagination, and shutting down democratic possibilities in education and the larger society. In direct contrast, radical consciousness, nurtured by critical dialogue, compels us to open the field to an active and rigorous investigation beyond simply our intuition or hunch—although Freire (1998) valued the significant contribution of these to learning. Rather than stopping there, however, he urged us to "build on our intuitions and submit them to methodological and rigorous analysis so that our curiosity becomes epistemological" (p. 48), and, in so doing, we uncover those actions that are in the service of transformation and a truly just world.

Thus, Freire proposed dialogue as a terrain of complexities, uncertainties, and ambiguities, where we must risk losing the old definitions of ourselves and the world, in order that we might reinvent it in ways that affirm the social agency and empowerment of the most oppressed. He anticipated that through dialogue students and teachers would enter a critical interrogation of unexamined assumptions and commonsense notions, for example, about why people are poor, or homeless, or unemployed, or incarcerated, or have dropped out of school. As well, they then may challenge pre-packaged and recycled solutions to poverty.

Such interrogations are important, given commonsensical assumptions of poverty based on oppressive myths—myths that ascribe superiority, entitlement, or privilege to those granted full subjecthood, under policies and practices that both conserve and reproduce racialized, patriarchal, heterosexual, and ableist relations of labor and marketplace desires, under the hegemony of capitalism. Paulo's decolonizing approach, on the other hand, requires that we confront misguided loyalties to economic values that normalize or mythicize abject poverty, unjust meritocracies, unprecedented incarceration, perpetual war, and a host of other economically bound conditions of human suffering.

Indispensability of Resistance

"What is essential is that learners . . . maintain alive the flame of resistance that sharpens their curiosity and stimulates their capacity to risk."

—Paulo Freire (1998)

To counter social and material oppression, Paulo looked to the indispensability of resistance. Stanley Aronowitz (1989), in his introduction to Freire's *Pedagogy of Freedom*, wrote: "Freire holds that a humanized society requires cultural freedom, the ability of the individual to choose values and rules of conduct that violate conventional social norms" (p. 19). But, of course, to *violate conventional social norms* entails that, by necessity, resistance or dissent have a central place in democratic life. Hence, student resistance in the classroom, for example, merits critical engagement, in that it plays an important role in the process of problem-posing dialogue and, hence, the development of consciousness. Rather than adversarial or problematic to the democratic construction of knowledge, resistance serves as a meaningful antecedent to the evolution of political consciousness.

Freire (1983) believed that no problem or act of resistance can be resolved by ignoring, dismissing, or squelching resistance or opposition without falling into authoritarianism. Instead, what we as teachers must learn to do is to cultivate and nurture dialogue in ways that create new fields of possibility large enough to welcome and navigate the tensions generated by resistance. This enhances the field from which students can launch their energies into emancipatory directions of inquiry, through critique and thoughtful engagement. It is this pedagogical response to resistance that most supports the communal evolution of radical consciousness, in that transformation is made possible through a collective democratic process of participation, voice, solidarity, and action that forges our communal reinvention of the world. Nevertheless, Freire (1994) argued adamantly that "A more critical understanding of the situation of oppression does not yet liberate the oppressed. But the revelation is a step in the right direction. Now the person who has this new understanding can engage in a political struggle with others for the transformation of the concrete conditions in which oppression prevails" (p. 24). Freire's concept of radicalization is also found herein.

Radicalization

"A more critical understanding of the situation of oppression does not yet liberate the oppressed. But the revelation is a step in the right direction. Now the person who has this new understanding can engage in a political struggle for the transformation of the concrete conditions in which oppression prevails."

—Paulo Freire (1994)

This to say that despite his overarching emphasis on the role of social relationships in the formation of critical consciousness, Freire recognized that each individual must also find within themselves and in communion with others that decisive point in their lived historical process that signals their radicalization, as an imperative of emancipatory life. This to say, political consciousness and a commitment to action cannot be transferred, in a banking mode, to students or communities, no matter how difficult the conditions of oppression might be. Freire (1970) addressed this point in speaking to the question of liberation as a critical form of praxis.

Liberation is a praxis: the action and reflection of men and women upon their world in order to transform it. Those truly committed to the cause of liberation can accept neither the mechanistic concept of consciousness as an empty vessel to be filled, nor the use of banking methods of domination (propaganda, slogans—deposits) in the name of liberation. Those truly committed to liberation must reject the banking concept in its entirety, adopting instead a concept of women and men as conscious beings, and consciousness, as consciousness intent upon the world (Freire, 1970, p.79).

To better comprehend the power and possibilities of emancipatory consciousness requires that we retain in place the dialectical qualities that underpin this process. More specifically, we radicalize, and are radicalized, through emancipatory relationships of political struggle with one another. This, however, does not collapse the individual into the communal, or the communal into the individual, in that each has a field of sovereignty and autonomy that is brought to bear, in the forging of radical consciousness. Rather than cogs in the great wheel of revolution or the historical process of evolution, we are, in fact, creators and co-creators of life—whether we participate passively through inaction and submission or bring forth critical impulses for liberation to bear upon the social and material structures that oppress our existence.

However, an ever-present question in the process of radicalization is how we make the radical option. Freire (1983) believed that the ethical man or woman "who makes a radical option" neither denies another the right to choose nor imposes that choice upon another. However, radicals do have "the duty, imposed by love, to react against the violence . . . in a situation in which the excessive power of a few leads to the dehumanization of all" (pp. 10–11). Unfortunately, it is precisely this human potential to know the world critically and to denounce injustice that is most corrupted by the lovelessness of oppression and the hostility of authoritarianism—a hostility that strived to disable the individual and collective participation and empowerment of those of us deemed political "renegades" or intellectual hoodlums, within the arena of the existing educational regime.

Instead, the radicalization of consciousness and sustained political struggle for democracy requires individuals who, through their commitment, political clarity, and love for the world, are capable of containing their arrant impulses and desires associated with unjust privilege and the internalization of oppression. Only in this way can we begin to move away from self-destructive behaviors or forms of resistance that betray our yearning for freedom. Further, Freire believed that both reason and human compassion must inform an emancipatory educational process; but this speaks to a reason and compassion born from a bodily and spiritual engagement with the world, rather than from prescribed forms of shallow sentimentalism.

Unquestionably, Freire recognized that if radical consciousness is indeed a journey or road to the unknown, then great courage, discipline, and commitment are required to denounce injustice and to remain ever present in the larger struggle for social and material transformations. Rather than a perspective that objectifies the outcome of democratic struggle as some definitive endpoint or transcendent utopia, Paulo implicitly came to know, through his own life, that the struggle for liberation is an ongoing revolutionary and evolutionary process, driven by a radical praxis, where ongoing reflection, voice, participation, action, and solidarity are fundamental ingredients to forging a culturally democratic and economically just world. So I close by invoking Paulo's (1998) words:

> Our comprehension of the future is not static but dynamic, and that we are convinced that our vocation for greatness and not mediocrity

> is an essential expression of the process of humanization in which we are inserted. These are the bases for nonconformity, for our refusal of destructive resignation in the face of oppression. It is not by resignation but by a capacity for indignation in the face of injustice that we are affirmed. (p. 74)

References

Aronowitz, S. (1989). Introduction. In P. Freire, *Pedagogy of freedom.* Rowman & Littlefield.

Darder, A. (2015). *Freire & education.* Routledge.

Davis, R. (1981). Education for awareness: A talk with Paulo Freire. In R. Mackie (Ed.), *Literacy & revolution* (pp. 57–69). Continuum.

Freire, P. (1970). *Pedagogy of the oppressed.* Continuum.

Freire, P. (1983). *Education for critical consciousness.* Seabury Press.

Freire, P. (1994). *Pedagogy of hope: Reliving Pedagogy of the Oppressed.* Continuum.

Freire, P. (1998). *Pedagogy of freedom: Ethics, democracy and civic courage.* Rowman & Littlefield.

Horton, M., & Freire, P. (1990). *We make the road by walking: Conversations on education and social change.* Temple University Press.

Endnotes

[1] This speech is based on excerpts from Antonia Darder (2015).

[2] *Prise de conscience* is here understood as the raising of consciousness or conscious realization.

CHAPTER ELEVEN

Revolution as Dialectical, Communal Praxis:

A Response to Antonia Darder

Lilia D. Monzó

Antonia Darder is a brilliant dialectician and master of radical and provocative politics. In "Freire and the Politics of Radical Consciousness" (Chapter Ten herein), Darder challenges us to engage Freire's work deeply and dialectically, negating the false binaries that develop through relations of domination and specifically under capitalist production and which have often, wittingly and unwittingly, infiltrated our radical politics. Focusing specifically on the development of a radical consciousness, Darder breaks the illusion of dismemberment and isolation that alienates us from ourselves and each other and shines light on our communal nature as human beings. As such she demonstrates that it is in the process of acting in communion with others to transform oppressive conditions that we develop the radical consciousness necessary to pave a path to freedom.

In this response essay, I elaborate on the false binaries that Darder posits, and I draw on Marx's concept of absolute negativity as a path to liberation. I attempt to breathe life into her arguments with examples that demonstrate that these are not utopian concepts but social relations that exist in this world, diminished under a cloud of oppression that triumphs through their negation. That they do exist is a testament to the critical hope that she, in honor of Freire, reinvents.

Bringing Our Whole Selves

Critical consciousness as transformational praxis has, perhaps unwittingly, been taken up through Cartesian disembodied notions of "rational" thought, such that even as we engage in praxis, which necessarily demands our whole *selves* in community with others, we continue to neglect those aspects that are at the core of not only praxis, but our very humanity. Darder reminds us that Freire's radical consciousness negated the alienation of our human faculties:

> This is particularly evident in *Pedagogy of Freedom*, when Freire (1998) asserts that "What is important in teaching is not the mechanical repetition of this or that gesture but a comprehension of the value of sentiments, emotions, and desires ... and sensibility, affectivity, and intuition" (p. 48). This powerful assertion of the value of our human faculties, beyond our reason, in the struggle for our liberation is a hallmark of Paulo Freire's pedagogy of love. (Darder, Chapter Ten herein)

Here Darder's focus is in bringing back those human qualities—emotions—that we have been socialized to hide, to quiet, and to detach from because a "common sense" has been established in the Gramscian sense. This "common sense" has us believe that emotions interfere with some presumed objective rational criticality. Darder attempts to awaken us to the fact that our dehumanization is tied to this dismembering. Regardless of our tendency to speak or act on our emotions and affectivity, we are beings that *feel* love, pain, desire, and anger in both sensual and emotional ways. Our feelings, thoughts, and actions are highly interrelated. And our moral compass, which guides our sense of justice, stems from a spiritual dimension that need not be religious but certainly cannot be fully grasped in the realm of "observable facts."

While many of us have been socialized to the "irrationality" of emotions, intuition, and spirituality, such that we make claims to "objective" truths and are expected to engage in our work "professionally" to such an extent that many people have difficulty expressing their emotion, most of us know that—try as we might—our feelings influence most of our work, actions, and interactions. The problem arises when we fail to acknowledge this human aspect of ourselves and judge others to be subhuman for more openly displaying their emotions and their spiritual guidance.

Yet there are beautiful examples of what can happen when we bring our whole selves to engage the world and develop, for the most part, non-alienating relationships. We can evidence this in some mother-child relationships wherein mutual respect and love are built. Although often presumed "instinctual" as a function of the capitalist gender division of labor that devalues women and their presumed "woman's role," mothering brings forth most of our faculties simultaneously, including "cognitive" labor.

A radical consciousness, as Freire conceived it and as Darder articulates, brings these human qualities together to become so indignant at the world's inhumanities that we are moved to act, reflect, and change the world.

Elsewhere, Darder argues for the negation of narrow definitions of science that reject our spiritual dimension and embrace political grace, which she defines as "a collective spiritual dimension that must manifest and unfold within our pedagogical and political praxis of community, if we are to genuinely extend our criticality beyond limiting and narrow allegiance to Western precepts of rationality" (Darder, 2016, para. 3). As I note elsewhere (Monzó, 2019):

> [Darder's] point here is that it is in the process of our political project for liberation that political grace emerges. This is critical because she does not let us off the hook by suggesting that political grace comes forth to propel us to act. On the contrary, it is we, as human agents, who create the spiritual connection that develops into political grace. (p. 267)

This spiritual connection can also enhance the process of conscientização.

The Self in Relation to the World

Reaching back to Freire's roots in Marx's philosophy of revolution, I recognize these feelings and the social conditions from which they emerge as social relations (Marx, 1977). From this view, who we are and how any one of us engages in the world is not an individual process, but one that develops socially and in community. Consider Eric Fromm's (1976) brilliant hypothesis that social processes, which develop in engagement with others, including loving and learning, have become, under commodity production, things to be possessed by individuals—in other words, private property.

As Fromm critiques, these processes have become psychological ownership, held in the head. Under capitalism, with its fundamental goal of accumulation and its emphasis on competition, the amassing of money and things grants power and status and has come to define people's self-worth. However, in a society defined by the increasing impoverishment of greater and greater numbers of people, processes become commodified.

Yet we do not move in the world alone but in a web of social relations. Mikhail Bakhtin (1981) reminds us that language, as a meaning-making system, is not learned from a dictionary but in community. We engage with others first ventriloquizing, and later appropriating and transforming these meanings by filling them with our own intentions and purposes. Yet this is not a linear developmental process; rather, it is one that can become reversed and that is continuously revisited as we make sense of the world as social actors. As Darder reminds us:

> This, however, does not collapse the individual into the communal, or the communal into the individual, in that each has a field of sovereignty and autonomy that is brought to bear, in the forging of radical consciousness. Rather than cogs in the great wheel of revolution or the historical process of evolution, we are, in fact, creators and co-creators of life—whether we participate passively through inaction and submission or bring forth critical impulses for liberation to bear upon the social and material structures that oppress our existence. (Darder, Chapter Ten herein)

The web of social relations in which we participate under capitalism produces a host of oppressive conditions for the majority who work in service of a small capitalist class. This web creates devastating social, economic, and political inequalities and differential opportunity structures based on class, race, Indigeneity, gender, sexuality, religion, and other antagonisms. In the Hegelian sense that the positive is always contained in the negative, this antagonistic web of social relations has also produced the basis for the development of communal formations that rally around the same social conditions of oppression and exploitation. These communities offer each other support and seek to change conditions. It is the conditions of necessary transformation that mediate and provide social relations and that inspire a collective hope and faith in each other and in our ability to create real change for the better. It is in and through these communal spaces and processes of transformation that, as Darder argues, radical consciousness is developed—it is not an individual process, not only a social relation, but a communal relation.

We see evidence that communal spaces for social transformation are springing up everywhere, some more and some less critical. The most salient, long-lasting examples are the Zapatistas of Chiapas, Mexico, who rose up on the day of the signing of NAFTA in 1994 and shortly thereafter won their autonomous existence. The Zapatistas have changed themselves and their social conditions through communal democratic processes.

Class and Race: In Support of Capitalist Production

Darder also engages the dialectical relation between consciousness and the material world, which is so important to Freire's concept of critical consciousness. Donaldo Macedo (2000) has importantly critiqued the too-common domestication of Freire's work into some version of "good teaching methods." These methods remain commensurate with capitalist production, or perhaps attempt to change specific social conditions abstracted from their relation to class. Darder (2002) emphatically denounces this domestication.

Freire's work was:

> "unabashedly grounded in Marxist-socialist thought. Without question, when Freire spoke of the 'ruling class' or the 'oppressors,' he was referring to historical class distinctions and class conflict within the structure of capitalist society—capitalism was the root of domination . . . . However for Freire, the struggle against economic domination could not be waged effectively without a humanizing praxis that could both engage the complex phenomena of class struggle and effectively foster the conditions for critical social agency among the masses." (p. 39)

Consciousness as a subjective reason (dialectically, this involves thinking and feeling) and the material objective world are in every aspect in continuous interaction, each a vital aspect of the other. The appearance of a binary is a mere illusion. Darder explains Freire's position:

> . . . he spoke to an emancipatory consciousness that arises through an organic process of human engagement, which requires human interactions that nurture our emancipatory relationship with the world. Only when we understand the dialectic relationship between consciousness and the world, "that is, when we know that we don't have a consciousness here and the world there; but, on the contrary, when both of them, the objectivity and the subjectivity, are incarnating dialectically, is it possible to understand what conscientização is, and to comprehend the role of consciousness in the liberation of humanity." (Darder, quoted in Davis, 1981, p. 62)

A devastating phenomenon that stems from this false binary is the antagonism and division that exists among scholars and activists whose work focuses on either class or race. While these are different structures of oppression, they are dialectically related, with each structure contributing to the maintenance and manifestations of the other. While class is often depicted as a material reality, it is maintained through ideologies that support the status quo and can be changed through a collective or communal class consciousness. In a similar vein, racism is often depicted as ideational reality, a consciousness that embeds stereotypes and fosters negative ideologies of the other, abstracted out of the material conditions that both led to and perpetuate it.

Our "tendency" to see the world through a set of binaries is not "natural" or "rational," but a product of histories of production processes that function through relations of domination across multiple axes that serve the ruling classes. These tendencies are learned in community and larger societal structures. Challenging them will require a collective communal process of radical consciousness that develops in the process of transformation. It is thus critical to examine what is referred to as a communal process, for it is more than merely working in larger groups.

Absolute Negativity

Absolute negativity is the resolution of the Hegelian dialectic. According to Hegel (1977), the source of unfreedoms lies in an internal contradiction, one negative and one positive, which is resolved by striking down the negative and allowing the positive to flourish. This is the first negation. However, this does not in itself dissolve the contradiction or produce a new and positive path, as the structure within which the antagonism was created remains. A second negation is necessary to challenge the existing structure altogether, unify, and present a new and creative step forward. Hegel perceived this process at the level of consciousness. However, freedom cannot be achieved at the level of consciousness alone.

Marx understood the significance of the dialectic but sought to develop a philosophy of revolution that would lead to freedom on both the material ideational planes. For Marx, freedom must be sought dialectically—in body and mind, objectively and subjectively. The process of becoming free on both these planes must be recognized as one process—a unity of presumed opposites (like idealism and materialism) wherein our consciousness is liberated in the process of developing freedom from material constraints.

Hegel's (1816) understanding of development and evolution in history is crucial to our goal of freedom, for it recognizes that what comes next is always held within that which came first. He stated: "To hold fast the positive in its negative, and the content of the presupposition in the result, is the most important part of rational cognition" (§1795).

The significance of this theory, as Marx recognized, is that we do not need to create freedom out of nothing. The positive lies dormant within the negative, and it will evolve through the struggle to negate the negative in our society. A step in the path to freedom is to recognize that we are not alone and to negate the ways in which we are partitioned into separate and distinct parts of ourselves, which includes our subjective and objective selves, as well as the isolation and individualism, which we are led to believe is natural. We are social beings, always unfinished, who develop when we engage our minds, emotions, and bodies in communion with others in the process of shaping our world.

In Community: Walking with Grace

Darder argues that it is in this process of engaging the world in communion with others that we develop the radical consciousness to change the world. That is, it is in the process of acting on conditions of injustice with people who face these social conditions that we come to see oppression as a structural phenomenon and to develop indignation, solidarity, and to humanize ourselves and each other. This is not a process that can be parsed out into discrete aspects of thinking, feeling, and acting. We engage in transformation with all aspects of ourselves and grow more human as we engage with our *whole* selves.

Communion and community take on a meaning that is much deeper, more spiritual, and more emotional than merely working toward shared goals. Communion and a communal project is one wherein people are "all in" with others. They share not only goals and strategies but hold a deep understanding about the specific impact of social conditions on the other, see them as fully human, and develop solidarity, which is a commitment to the other. Communal relations are not about friendships or caring for individuals, but about a love for humanity, a recognition of our interdependence, and a commitment to justice.

To be in communion or to develop communal relations is a grand goal, but a necessary one if we are to take on the mighty monsters that inhabit this world. Drawing on Darder's work on political grace, I would argue that when we build actual community, we move through the world with grace—a spiritual confidence born out of the factual and faith assertion that we are not alone and, at the same time, we make a collective one. Freedom is everyone's quest and everyone's right.

References

Bakhtin, M.M. (1981). *The dialogic imagination: Four essays*. Holquist, M. (Ed.); trans. Caryl Emerson and Michael Holquist. University of Texas Press.

Darder, A. (2002). *Reinventing Paulo Freire: A pedagogy of love*. Westview Press.

Darder, A. (2016). Political grace and revolutionary critical pedagogy. *Rizoma Freireano*, no. 21. http://www.rizoma-freireano.org/articles-2121/political-grace-21

Darder, A. (2021). The presence of Paulo Freire at Chapman University (Chapter Ten in the present volume). Myers Education Press.

Davis, R. (1981). Education for awareness: A talk with Paulo Freire. In R. Mackie (Ed.), *Literacy & revolution* (pp. 57–69). Continuum.

Fromm, E. (1976). *To have or to be*. Bloomsbury.

Hegel, G.W.F. (1816). *The science of logic: The absolute idea*. Marxists Internet Archive. https://www.marxists.org/reference/archive/hegel/works/hl/hlabsolu.htm

Hegel, G.W.F. (1977). *Hegel's Phenomenology of spirit*. Oxford University Press.

Macedo, D. (2000). Introduction. In P. Freire, *Pedagogy of the oppressed, 30th anniversary edition* (pp. 11–27). Bloomsbury.

Marx, K. (1977). *Capital, Vol. I*, trans. Ben Fowkes. Vintage Books.

Monzó, L.D. (2019). *A revolutionary subject: Pedagogy of women of color and indigeneity*. Peter Lang.

CHAPTER TWELVE

Liberation Through Love:
Things Freire and My Mama Taught Me

Kimberly A. White-Smith

In Antonia Darder's essay "Freire and the Politics of Radical Consciousness" (Darder, 2021, Chapter Ten herein), she writes: ". . . critical consciousness, although it takes place in and emerges out of the expressed lived histories of each individual, cannot evolve and transform in the absence of others." Before the Civil Rights Act of 1964, people of color, and Blacks in particular, were collectively committed to the struggle for liberation and equality. Intrinsic to organizing coalitions to create systemic change was the development of a Black Critical Consciousness movement (Carmichael & Hamilton, 1992). Evidence of the ways in which segregated communities coalesce can be found in the power of Black churches such as the Southern Christian Leadership Conference, the influence of the Student Non-violent Coordinating Committee, and the rise of the Black Panther Party and the Nation of Islam. This drive for identity and awareness of the Black American fed the Civil Rights Movement. This essay is rooted in my frustration with contemporary apathy toward the plight of Black Americans and the anti-Black sentiment that serves to normalize state-sanctioned violence and oppressive policies against Black bodies.

My interest in actively participating in the struggle to emancipate Black people—my people—from the perils of a society built on the ideology of White supremacy and the enslavement of African people began when I was 12 years old. I recall the first time I engaged in a serious conversation with my mother about her life before *Brown v. Board of Education* (1954) and the desegregation laws that soon followed. We were driving past the old, burned-out Goodyear factory off Central Avenue in East Los Angeles on our way to Waddy's Barbershop to get my brother a haircut. My Mama began to talk about her experiences growing up in the South during the time that Jim Crow Laws were in full effect. I turned to look at her and said, "It must have been hard, Mama, not being allowed to go to good schools, not being able to eat at nice restaurants." Mama hummed, "No, no, It wasn't hard, baby. *Desegregation*—now that was hard. Living in our communities, we felt safe. Everyone kept an eye out on their neighbors' kids, not just their own. And the teachers knew their stuff, and they made us learn." A broad smile grew across Mama's face, and she began to recite a verse from the Langston Hughes poem *I Too*."

Mama went on to say, "Our teachers cared about us. They knew us. They were a part of our community; they were a part of our lives. They helped us understand that to make it in this world, we had to be three times better than the White person standing next to you. Our teachers knew our opportunities would be few, so they made sure we were prepared. We respected our teachers. Education was important. We had our own doctors, our own lawyers. We had restaurants with the best food—collard greens with fatback, ham hocks and black-eyed peas, oxtails, and hot water cornbread. Desegregation—now that was the monster that tore our community apart."

I was in the 6th grade. We had just studied the Civil Rights Movement and desegregation. My mother, Cleopatra White, was born in 1919, and she had told me many stories about Texarkana, Arkansas, where she grew up. Until that time I could not appreciate the significance of her words. I learned in school that segregation was a horrible evil that robbed Black children of the opportunity to obtain a high-quality education. However, my mother and her contemporaries, albeit forced by segregation laws, engaged in a process that engendered a communal knowledge base and value system. These incorporated and embraced the gifts cultivated in the Black community, preparing those in her community to navigate challenging situations while maintaining a positive identity of self.

Drawing on her schooling experiences, she described a curriculum that was rigorous and rich in the literature relevant to Black culture. Her teachers were a part of the community and interacted with caregivers and families regularly. All members of the community took responsibility to support and guide all the children. These practices are currently described in the education literature as being culturally responsive or culturally sustaining (e.g.,

Allen & White-Smith, 2014; Ball, 2000; Cooper, 2009; Delpit, 1995; Grant & Sleeter, 2006; Ladson-Billings, 1994; Paris, 2012; Paris & Alim, 2014; White-Smith, 2012).

In Darder's essay in the present volume (Chapter Ten), "Freire and the Politics of Radical Consciousness," she discusses the process of conscientização. It reminded me of this moment in the car with my mother. Our conversation around my limited and narrow understanding of the strengths of Black communities during segregation was an opportunity to experience a critical awakening. It was a turning point in my development as a student and as a young Black person. I thirsted to delve deeper into our complicated history so I could use this knowledge to act upon the injustices that my people and I endured. Darder states: "The struggle for change begins . . . at that moment when human beings become both critically aware and fully intolerant of the oppressive conditions in which we find ourselves; and from there, transgress toward new ways of knowing and being in the world."

Prince Charles: My Road to Black Critical Consciousness Reimagined

Based on my conversation with my mother, it is apparent that as a child, I was indoctrinated via the formal and informal channels of education through White-washed curriculum, teachers, television, and the media to believe that schools devoid of White children were inferior; thus, the struggle for the right to go to White schools and live in White spaces was essential. However, what my mother described of her schooling experience ran contrary to those beliefs. The deficit perspectives I harbored about my community blinded me from recognizing the cultural wealth and assets that existed amid egregious human rights violations designed to perpetuate White supremacy and societal inequality. I sought to correct my miseducation of younger years when I attended college, where I was introduced to the idea of critical consciousness through the writings of Frantz Fanon. In his book *White Skin, Black Masks* (1967), Fanon discusses his role in leading his Black patients to "*consciousnessize*" (p. 170). He describes it as an awakening to the fact that society needs to propagate a system that induces a sense of inferiority and a desire to be White in Black people so that Whites can maintain unearned advantages, power, and wealth. In order to regain mental health, Fanon argued, Blacks must embrace their identity and push to change the real problem, which is institutionalized inequality. He stated that

> the Black man should no longer have to be faced with the dilemma "whiten or perish," but must become aware of the possibility of existence; . . . if society creates difficulties for him because of his color, if I see in his dreams the expression of an unconscious desire to change color, my objective will not be to dissuade him by advising him to 'keep his distance'; on the contrary . . . my objective will be to enable him to choose action (or passivity) with respect to the real source of the conflict, i.e., the social structure. (p. 171)

It is essential to acknowledge that the activists who worked toward desegregation were absolutely on the right side of history, and I am not advocating for legalized racial segregation; unfortunately, the wealth and opportunity gaps prevalent in our country have firmly cemented de facto segregation. However, we must be vigilant in understanding that the struggle for equality does not rest on the shoulders of a few talented individuals. Our strength and success as a people have always come through collective action and collective activism. It is easy to buy into the Eurocentric and gendered ideology of "the hero or the heroine," as we have done for individual Black Americans like Dr. Martin Luther King, Jr., or Rosa Parks. Society intentionally tends to forget and fails to teach that these individuals were not exceptional but part of a collective of activists. As Darder explains, "we don't need the Lone Ranger or superman to save us—instead, we need one another, if we are to genuinely live critically and democratically" (Chapter Ten herein). Sister Rosa Parks did not just decide to sit down on the bus one day because she was tired. It was part of a strategic plan that had been thought out and implemented by the group. Dr. King had become frustrated because the movement was stalled. If it were not for the children of Birmingham, Alabama, who on May 2–5, 1963, put their beautiful brown bodies between Bull Connor's fire hoses and the liberation of our community, JFK would not have so readily signed the Civil Rights Act of 1964.

Critical pedagogy has always been crucial in the development, support, and anchoring of the practice of teaching and learning. The practice serves to illuminate the limitations of a mono-worldview and strives to build an enhanced identity and perspective shaped and changed through dialogue and interactions with people, knowledge, and experiences.

I recall a conversation with my brother, Prince Charles, about his son and his experiences with schooling that greatly influenced my understanding of learning emancipatory praxis. Prince said:

> If you want to make it in this world, you need education. I want him to hit them books and get some brains like his auntie. But this mess is hard. He needs to know Dad ain't no superman. He needs to get his butt on the bus in the morning and get to school. He skipped school the other day, and I had to tear that butt up, but I tell you, that whipping I gave him ain't nothing compared to the whipping the world gonna give him, if he gets out in them streets and ain't got nothing in his head and no plan in life. (Prince Charles, personal communication, 2011)

The above interaction between my brother and me encapsulates the unspoken pressure and responsibility that Black parents feel to protect their children from the consequences of not conforming to societal expectations for Black people as defined by White people. It also surmises the role schools play in perpetuating the oppression of marginalized students. The "whipping" described in the scenario by Prince is not a moment of anger or rage from a parent to a child, but an example of the terror and dread that he as a Black parent feels, and which is the result of a world that seeks to crush his son through a system of institutionalized bigotry and racial oppression.

According to a study by the National Academy of Sciences (Edwards et al., 2019), Black men are 2.5 times more likely to be killed by police than are White men in the United States. This fear for our children has persisted over the years, with documented examples of racial profiling, police brutality, and racially motivated violence.

Black men, women, boys, and girls, both cis- and transgender, have suffered and died in the charge of an unjust legal system. I start with a never-ending list of names: Breonna Taylor, Ahmaud Arbery, Tony McDade, Rekia Boyd, Sandra Bland, Michael Brown, Tamir Rice, Renisha McBride, Sheneque Proctor, Aura Rosser, Ronald Madison, Amadou Diallo, Steve Eugene Washington, Tyree Woodson, Alan Blueford, Dante Porter, James Bissette Ervin Jefferson, Ezell Ford, Levi Weaver, Oscar Grant, Rashad McIntosh, Qusean Whitten, Jon Ferrell, Eric Garner, Alonzo Ashley, Aaron Campbell, Sean Bell,

Laquan McDonald, Phillip Pannell, Ramarley Graham, Kimani Gray, Timothy Stansbury, Jr., Victor White, Armand Bennett, Miguel Benton, Victor Steen, Cameron Tillman, Orlando Barlow, Dane Scott, Patrick Dorismond, Jonathan Ferrell, Tavares McGill, Deion Fludd, Wendell Allen, Kendrec McDade, Derrick Williams, Carey Smith-Viramontes, John Crawford III, and Timothy Russell are only a few.

The #BlackLivesMatter movement was born from the ashes of the heinous murder of 17-year-old Trayvon Martin while visiting his father in Florida. George Zimmerman, who was not a police officer, but a neighborhood watch coordinator, was—incredulously—set free by the judicial system. This movement, conceived collaboratively by three queer Black womyn—Alicia Garza, Patrisse Cullors, and Opal Tometi—was the beginning of a new form of Black Critical Consciousness. According to Alicia Garza (2016), "Black Lives Matter is an ideological and political intervention in a world where Black lives are systematically and intentionally targeted for demise. It is an affirmation of Black folks' contributions to this society, our humanity, and our resilience in the face of deadly oppression" (p. 23). The movement harkened to what Darder echoes from Freire as the "emancipatory consciousness that arises through an organic process of human engagement, which requires human interactions that nurture our emancipatory relationship with the world" (p. 2).

The #BlackLivesMatter movement came to life at a time when the repugnance of anti-Blackness was hidden beneath the veneer of a Black president and a façade of equality. As #BlackLivesMatter gained traction and attention, so did those individuals and organizations who sought to detract, subjugate, and hijack the movement. Both those factions and the media reframed a movement of love and solidarity for Black people as militant, violent, and anti-White. What was good for Black folx was perceived as detrimental and dangerous to the foundation of White society, at least until the COVID-19 pandemic struck. The devastating virus that literally brought the world to a halt has marred the year 2020. With orders to stay at home, fighting this pandemic forced businesses, schools, and entertainment venues to close.

On May 25, 2020, in Minneapolis, Minnesota, the nation witnessed, via cell phone video recordings and later body cam footage, Police Officer Derek Chauvin place his knee on the neck of George Floyd for 8 minutes and 46 seconds and extinguish the brilliant light of yet another Black soul. Once again the United States was forced to look in the mirror and see the ugly scars of a society built on White racial hegemony and the blood of Black people. In that moment the collective consciousness of the Black community awoke and, in droves, Black people—along with others who condemned the heinous murder—took to the streets in protest. The #BlackLivesMatter movement became even more relevant in light of the sheer audacity of killing Brother Floyd in front of a crowd of people and on camera. Continuing to conceptualize White racial hegemony solely as a privilege or unearned societal advantage veils the destructive power leveraged by Whites to dismantle and eradicate the stories, the accomplishments, and the very lives of Black, Indigenous, People of Color (Cabrera, 2017; Cabrera, 2018; Leonardo, 2004; Matias, 2016).

Leonardo (2004) wrote that "the conditions of White supremacy make White privilege possible. In order for White racial hegemony to saturate everyday life, it has to be secured by a process of domination, or those acts, decisions, and policies that White subjects perpetrate on people[s] of color" (p. 137). This is evidenced not only in the sanctioned murder of Blacks by police with impunity, but also by the way in which White women consistently weaponize Whiteness to threaten Black civilians (Earick, 2018; Nir, 2020).

Until you do right by me: The courage to stand with those you oppress

The belief that every breath a Black person takes is an affront to White society is perplexing, and it pushes me to think of how we can begin to engage in the practice of liberatory consciousness to save the lives of Black people. Our voices, our hair, our clothes, our skin, our lives, our existence are manifestations of the perseverance and spirit of our ancestors and a means for others to limit our freedoms and police our bodies. The pretense that we live in a "woke," critically conscious, or post-racial society (Hamel, 2016) is inaccurate at best. Freire (1970) posits that critical consciousness is a continuous journey, and we are continuously evolving. Darder (2021, herein) asserts that it is a communal and democratic process. The collective trauma that Blacks are experiencing as a people in this moment is not only painful, but triggers the generational, emotional, and physical trauma we have inherited. I posit that building a personal and professional practice of critical consciousness rooted in love that is both radical and transformative has the power and potential to heal as we resist and demand change. I have been encouraged and renewed by the work of Black women centering love as a means both to care for those engaged in the labor of emancipation and as a tool to abolish systems of oppression (Love, 2019; Paris, 2020; Sealey-Ruiz, 2020; Annamma, 2018).

I call upon the reader to engage in Freire's (1970) concept of radical consciousness. How committed are you to the cause? Would you step out of your comfort zone to affirmatively and publically stand in solidarity with those who are oppressed and devalued? For me, the most impactful scene from the movie *The Color Purple* (Spielberg, 1985) is between the antagonist Mister and the protagonist Celie, whom he subjugated, humiliated, and tortured. He looked at her and said, "You can curse nobody. Look at you. You're black, you're poor, you're ugly, you're a woman, you're nothing at all!" She simply looked at him and responded, "Until you do right by me, everything you even think about gonna fail!"

References

Allen, Q., & White-Smith, K.A. (2014). "Just as bad as prisons": The challenge of dismantling the school-to-prison pipeline through teacher and community education. *Equity and Excellence in Education*, 44, 259–279.

Annamma, S.A. (2018). *The pedagogy of pathologization: Dis/abled girls of color in the school-prison nexus*. Routledge.

Ball, A.F. (2000). Empowering pedagogies that enhance the learning of multicultural students. *Teachers College Record*, 102(6), 1006–1034.

Brown v. Board of Education, 347 U.S. 483 (1954). https://www.oyez.org/cases/1940-1955/347us483

Cabrera, N.L. (2017). White immunity: Working through the pedagogical pitfalls of privilege. *Journal Committed to Social Change on Race and Ethnicity*, 3(1), 74–86.

Cabrera, N.L. (2018). *White guys on campus: Racism, White immunity, and the myth of "post-racial" higher education*. Rutgers University Press.

Carmichael, S., & Hamilton, C. (1992). *Black power: The politics of liberation in America*. Vintage Books.

Cooper, C.W. (2009). Parent involvement, African American mothers, and the politics of educational care. *Equity & Excellence in Education*, 42(4), 379–394.

Delpit, L. (1995). *Other people's children: Cultural conflict in the classroom*. The New Press.

Earick, M.E. (2018). We are not social justice equals: The need for White scholars to understand their Whiteness. *International Journal of Qualitative Studies in Education*, 31(8), 800–820.

Edwards, F., Lee, H., & Esposito, M. (2019, August). Risk of being killed by police use of force in the United States by age, race-ethnicity, and sex. *Proceedings of the National Academy of Sciences*, 116(34), 16793–16798; DOI: 10.1073/pnas.1821204116

Fanon, F. (1967). *Black skin, White Masks* (C. Markmann, Trans.; 1st edition). Grove Press. (1952)

Freire, P. (1970). *Pedagogy of the oppressed.* Continuum.

Garza, A. (2016). A herstory of the #BlackLivesMatter Movement. In J. Hobson (Ed.), *Are all the women still White? Rethinking race, expanding feminisms* (pp. 23–28). SUNY Press.

Grant, C.A., & Sleeter, C.E. (2006). *Turning on learning: Five approaches for multicultural teaching plans for race, class, gender and disability*, (4th ed). Jossey-Bass.

Hamel, A. (2016). The post-racial society is here. *Journal of Race & Policy*, 12(1), 54–55.

Hughes, Langston. "I, Too." Poetry Foundation. https://www.poetryfoundation.org/poems/47558/i-too

Ladson-Billings, G. (1994). *The dreamkeepers: Successful teachers of African American children* (1st ed.). Jossey-Bass.

Leonardo, Z. (2004). The color of supremacy: Beyond the discourse of "White privilege." *Educational Philosophy and Theory*, 36(2), 137–152.

Love, B.L. (2019). *We want to do more than survive: Abolitionist teaching and the pursuit of educational freedom.* Beacon Press.

Matias, C. (2016). "Why do you make me hate myself?": Re-teaching Whiteness, abuse, and love in urban teacher education. *Teaching Education*, 27(2), 194–211.

Nir, S.M. (2020, June 14). *How 2 lives collided in Central Park, rattling the nation.* The New York Times. https://www.nytimes.com/2020/06/14/nyregion/central-park-amy-cooper-christian-racism.html

Paris, D. (2012). Culturally sustaining pedagogy: A needed change in stance, terminology, and practice. *Educational Researcher*, 41(3), 93–97.

Paris, D., & Alim, H.S. (2014). What are we seeking to sustain through culturally sustaining pedagogy? A loving critique forward. *Harvard Educational Review*, 84(1), 85–100.

Paris, R. (2020). How "An open letter of love to Black students: #BLACKLIVESMATTER" came to be. In A.E. Shield, D. Paris, R. Paris, & T. San Pedro (Eds.), *Education in movement spaces: Standing Rock to Chicago Freedom Square* (pp. 119–132). Routledge.

Sealey-Ruiz, Y. (2020). *Love from the vortex & other poems.* Kaleidoscope Vibrations, LLC.

Spielberg, S. (1985). *The color purple.* Warner Bros.

White-Smith, K.A. (2012). Beyond instructional leadership: The lived experiences of principals in successful urban schools. *Journal of School Leadership*, 22(1), 6–25.

Section Four: Questions and Activity

Questions

1. Darder writes about conscientization and its living expression in action. In what ways are any of these elements reflected in your own life as a student, activist, and/or scholar?
2. How does Monzó's call to consciously engage as our "whole selves" highlight ongoing approaches to critical and dialogical engagement with the world?
3. What does White-Smith's chapter reveal about critical consciousness? How does your learning from her chapter relate to the current socio-political context?

Activity: Concept Cloud

Each author has revealed that conscientization takes place in multiple, concrete historical and human contexts. In this activity, we ask you to conceptualize critical consciousness by creating an individual concept cloud. After the mapping process, we ask that you engage in collective dialogue based on your concept cloud.

- **Concept Cloud:**
  - Place the word "critical consciousness" at the center of the page.
  - Next, write down key terms from each chapter around the central concept.
  - Examine the collection of terms to see what is missing and/or contribute your own terms to describe this concept.
- **Collective Dialogue based on the Concept Cloud:**
  - What is your understanding or experience of critical consciousness, and how is it informed by the contexts of your own life?
  - How is your praxis of critical consciousness informed by the contexts of your own life, and how does such praxis inform these same contexts?
  - How does critical consciousness both inform, and is informed by, your praxis?

Section Five

CHAPTER THIRTEEN

Re-Inventing Paulo Freire Ethically

DONALDO MACEDO

> *"A day after New York City came up with a $1,000.00 Bagel, a local restaurateur unveiled a $27,000 Chocolate Sundae today, setting a Guinness World Record for the most expensive dessert."*
>
> —*Business News* May 14, 2009

LET ME FIRST THANK Suzi SooHoo, Tom Wilson, Anaida Colón-Muñiz, Lilia Monzó, and Peter McLaren for their vision, hard work, and commitment to promoting Paulo Freire's leading ideas and ideals, and for making this conference possible. A special thanks goes to Dean Don Cardinal, who understands that the future of education lies with social justice, evident in his invaluable support for the Paulo Freire Democratic Project. Crucially, the project responds to the ideas that students "ain't going" to read if they are hungry, "ain't doing" math if they are homeless, and "ain't racing" to the top—despite Obama's promise—if they are growing up under cemented histories of racism, sexism, and other forms of oppression. Tragically, many see today's inequities—and the oppressive power relations that undergird them—as natural (or at least inevitable). There was no outrage when a Manhattan restaurant asked diners to pay a stunning $27,000 for a chocolate sundae while paying its workers—who are notably women, Afro-Americans, and Latinas—much less for a year of their labor. In the wake of the Occupy Movement, little outrage has emerged in response to this kind of severe inequity.

Yet, I want to argue, we should be—as Freire would say—"justly angry." We should be furious that one sector of society can afford to spend, in a night, what another makes in a year. We should be furious that rather than correcting this inequality by, for example, installing redressive measures to support the success of all youth, we popularly press students to "race [against each other] to the top" (https://www2.ed.gov/programs/racetothetop/index.html), even though many children have so few resources they can hardly start "the race" in the first place. While our society—the richest in the world—rewards hedge fund managers with endless disposable income, it sentences millions of families to a nightmarish present characterized by homelessness and hopelessness. Unable to provide their children with a roof over their heads, they are forced to shuttle them from shelter to shelter—homeless children whose bedrooms are often the back seats of cars and who often arrive at school sleepy, unwashed, and hungry, greeted by teachers who, ritualistically and unreflectively, sometimes require these homeless children to recite, in unison and with conviction, the phrase of the Declaration of Independence that promises "Life, Liberty and the Pursuit of Happiness"; homeless children who are cheated at an early age of a future and are left only with the possibility of prison or a career as working poor earning unlivable wages. The rapid expansion of the working poor and the shrinkage of the middle class mirrors, in so many ways, so-called Third World countries where the gulf between the ruling class and the working class is so visible and not hidden, as it is in the United States—an invisibility produced and reproduced through myths of a classless society believed even by those locked in segregated ghettos.

The Chapman *Paulo Freire Democratic Project*'s commitment to the radicality of Freire's philosophy, ideals, and pedagogy makes clear that teachers cannot and should not accommodate the inhumanity of exploitation, the relegation of millions of children to dire poverty, and the disposability of honest workers (who are being made increasingly redundant as the ruling class happily pays $10,000 for a martini with a "1.52-carat 'radiant' cut diamond" at the Algonquin Hotel in New York City. In encountering this painful context, those of us who consider ourselves Freireans need to feel indignation at the obscene greed and perverse consumerism of the era, indignation at the popular feeling that so many people are disposable, like non-white youth who are increasingly marginalized (indeed, criminalized) both within and outside of their classrooms.

Today's unsettling landscape of ever-increasing misery and exploitation demands a careful consideration of the related consequences of different kinds of scholarship and pedagogy, of their ability to foster or forestall oppression.

Of late, I have been haunted by a disturbing trend in contemporary scholarship: careerist abuses of Freirean theory. More specifically, I am talking about the kind of scholarship that claims to be critical and progressive while in fact working primarily to further the researcher's own crass careerist interests. That kind of scholarship reeks of *political and intellectual incoherence*. These scholars sacrifice their avowed political projects at the altar of individualism, driven by a blind careerism that often bleaches out the meaning of collective struggle, community engagement, honesty, solidarity, and humanism. Hence, a blind careerism is a by-product of a kind of *neoliberal intellectualism*—work that claims to foster freedom while really just bolstering its own elite (its writer)—work that doesn't really mend inequities but rather deepens them, and puts one (and clearly an already "privileged" one) ahead of the rest, given that this scholar has a voice at all, a voice he/she is using to speak *for*, not *with*, the communities he/she allegedly engages.

In many respects, these supposedly critical writers who never organically engage the communities they speak *for* other than as anthropological tourists, these so-called critical writers who have never set foot in inner city classrooms yet propose educational reforms, continue to produce *selfish scholarship* that remains linked to *colonial scholarship*. The latter refers to the history of colonizers "writing" those they worked to colonize, through scholarly studies. This undoubtedly continues today, sometimes subconsciously, for even well-intentioned researchers do not realize that they are "writing" the communities they study to the extent that the role of the researcher is to speak *for* and not *with* is just so normalized. It is a normalization that gives rise to academic pimping, a process that also normalizes scholars as *anthropological tourists* who are, invariably, incoherent intellectuals.

A boast that one is the resident leftist, while it may appear to be courageous, does not guarantee political coherence. And to be sure, as Amilcar Cabral (1973) would say, in denouncing economic exploitation, violence, and dehumanization, "it is not necessary to be courageous. It is enough to be honest" (p. 16). And to be honest is to see the obvious contradiction in the proud claim to be so far left and brag to be, for example, the resident Maoist at a university while, at the same time, refusing to de-Guccify bourgeois tastes and consumerist practices. Within this troubling context, honesty means, in part, denouncing both allegedly uncritical and critical educators who, in Freire's (1985) words, "treat the [the communities they] study as though [they] are not participants in it. In [their] celebrated [scholarly] impartiality, [they] might approach [the real communities] as if [they] were wearing 'gloves and masks' in order not to be contaminated or be contaminated by [them]."

In other words, when educators use communities as laboratories for their critical or acritical studies without ever developing an authentic communion with them, they are, in a sense, *academic pimps*. Worse yet, these scholars often abandon their anthropological tourism after the data is collected and the community members are, once more, relegated to the status of rats in a laboratory, creatures whose usefulness has a shelf life. This is the model of most academic researchers who, for example, would slum in Haiti to collect data for their studies and soon forget the human misery and dire poverty they left behind. Further, upon return, they usually avoid the Haitian communities that surround their universities. This kind of educator, critical or not, spends little time in communities and often sends his or her students to the community to collect data so they can become the experts and/or spokespeople—*representatives*—for the community with which they never interact.

In the face of this incoherent kind of scholarship, I want to think about how we might more thoughtfully engage Freire's work, in the interest of *true* liberation. More specifically, in more aptly putting Freire into practice, critical educators must always have the necessary intellectual coherence to understand the critical difference between, for example, writing about hunger and experiencing it, deploring violence and surviving it, and giving voice (often a kind of false benevolence) and being forced to be voiceless. A *coherent intellectual* must walk his/her talk and avoid the academification of oppression and the false generosity that accompanies it. He/she does not wear "gloves and masks" when working with community members, especially those who have been *othered* by virtue of their race, culture, class, ethnicity, and sexual orientation—and yet, a coherent intellectual is always careful when engaging individuals to recognize that one can never *fully* know the *Other*.

It is important to emphasize here that though coherent intellectuals work *with* community or schools and so engage *otherness*, they must always be vigilant not to engage *others* in ways that allow the scholar to "colonize" them, that lead intellectuals to participate in the problematic politics of "writing" others in their studies. By disposing of "gloves and masks," critical educators develop the necessary conviviality with economic deprivation that teaches them that poverty is not Ebola but a social construction—that poverty is not contagious but part of the architecture of a hierarchical capitalist class structure that they hypocritically denounce in their discourse but do not as readily renounce in their consumerist practice and their Guccified ways of being in a market-driven society. These educators invariably engage in the construction of human misery that they correctly condemn in their writings, making them at times what one may call "revolutionaries in silk underwear."

In order to avoid falling into a kind of Swiss cheese political project, one that is partially holed-out in areas by careerist ambition, critical educators should not opportunistically appropriate Freire, sloganizing him into their allegedly exotic (but really mechanistic) methods. Instead, critical, coherent educators should embrace Freire's wish to never import or export his ideas and ideals but to ethically *re-invent* them.

In considering how we might best ethically re-invent Paulo today, we could begin by reflecting on the role that his wife, Nita, played in inspiring his radical philosophy and pedagogy. Without the unconditional love they shared, without Nita's generosity, and without her loving refusal to let Paulo be commodified into a kind of Freire-industrial-complex, we would probably not be here today—or, at least, we would definitely not be talking about Paulo's insistence that to teach is to be ethical and that any form of intellectual endeavor without ethics is a pure intellectualist exercise. Without Nita, we would not have the gift of *Pedagogy of Freedom*—a book in which Paulo extensively discusses ethics.

According to Stanley Aronowitz (1998), this book is one of Paulo's best works. In it, Freire once again highlights that "a humanist society requires cultural autonomy, the ability of a person to choose values and rules that violate the unjust social norms and, a political and civil society requires a total participation of its inhabitants in all aspects of public life." (p. 19) According to Paulo, "Nita Freire not only re-inspired Freire to re-unleash his indignation and rebelliousness in a more direct and accessible manner, but she also influenced him to embrace 'a language that is more inviting, less dense, more poetic.'" (Macedo, 2013, p. 83). The last ten years of Paulo's life with Nita offer a strong lens through which we might appreciate what it meant for the author who gave us *Pedagogy of the Oppressed* to be in the world, with the world, and with others in the world. These years provide an opportunity to comprehend more deeply the origins and directives of Paulo's insistence that we must always think of history as suggesting possibility—a perspective that nearly eluded him upon the death of his first wife, Elza. I remember witnessing—alongside Antonia Darder and Tom Wilson—Paulo's almost tragic surrender to history after Elza's death, when he walked to the stage, greeted by an interminable standing ovation upon his first visit to the United States, invited by Tom to speak at UC Irvine. After a long silence following the applause, Paulo softly uttered: "I am sorry, but I cannot go on." His friends and the translator ushered him from the stage. Though he had made the long journey from Brazil to give a lecture that day, he was unable to deliver it.

Paulo's insistence that we view history as possibility was resurrected for me when I visited him in São Paulo a year later. I phoned him upon my arrival and, contrary to my expectation of listening to the Paulo without hope in a utopian possibility, his voice on the other end of the phone was beaming with joy and happiness. Paulo invited me to lunch that same day. When I arrived at his house, he introduced me to this hugely intelligent and elegant woman, Nita Araújo. Paulo was so passionate: he could not stop talking about Nita's fantastic and illuminating contributions to the history of Brazilian education.

When we sat down to eat, I noticed that Paulo was so zealous that he was even being a bit territorial, seeing to it that Nita sat next to him. During lunch, I realized that Paulo had again developed a coherence between his words, actions, and ideas. I vividly remembered what he had once shared with me: "to never let the child in you die." His playfulness with Nita, his loving smile when she spoke, and his almost clumsy attempt to hold her hand led me to believe that Paulo was crazy in love with her.

During his last visit to New York, months before his untimely death, he and I were walking on Lexington Avenue. I shared with him the fear we all experienced of losing him ten years earlier when he was unable to deliver the speech he had traveled to Irvine to give. I remember clearly that he stopped, put his hands gently on my shoulder, and told me in a very tender voice: "Yes, Donaldo. I was also afraid that I no longer wanted to live. What Nita gave me was fantastic! It was magical! Nita not only made me re-discover the joy of life, but she also taught me a very important lesson that I knew intellectually but had emotionally forgotten: that we must never forget that history always suggests possibility. It is always possible to love again." Paulo then added: "Nita not only taught me that it is always possible to love again, but she also gave me a new and renewed intellectual energy. *Pedagogy of Hope*, that encounter with *Pedagogy of the Oppressed*, could never have been written without Nita's inspiration. She is without a doubt one of the few people who truly and completely understands my thinking and my work. It is almost scary! Sometimes I feel that she knows my ideas better than I do."

The invitation to speak about my relationship with Paulo gives me another opportunity to thank him anew for having been in this world, for having zealously worked to transform its ugliness, and for insisting that, while change is difficult, it is *always* possible. It is always possible to make this world less discriminatory, more just, less dehumanizing, more humane. Crucially, Paulo reminds us that changing the world must always be anchored in a passionate, revolutionary love infused with "just anger," compassion, and unwavering hope. He always denounced the duplicity of educators who accommodate—educators who willingly embrace the social construction of "not seeing" to justify teaching on their knees. In response to his aggressive denunciation of the domesticated educator, Paulo simultaneously theorized an educational vision rooted in a permanent struggle against social injustice—a struggle that points to a future shaped by equity, humility, and love.

References

Aronowitz, S. (1998). Introduction. In P. Freire, *Pedagogy of freedom: Ethics, democracy, and civic courage*. Rowman & Littlefield.

Cabral, A. (1973). *Return to the source: Selected speeches of Amilcar Cabral*. Monthly Review Press.

Macedo, D. (2013). Situating Pedagogy of the Oppressed after Nita Freire. *International Journal of Critical Pedagogy* , 5(1), 82-100.

Freire, P., Giroux, H. A., & Macedo, D. P. (1985). *The politics of education: Culture, power, and liberation*. South Hadley, Mass: Bergin & Garvey.

CHAPTER FOURTEEN

Freire, Ethics, and Revolutionary Love:

A Response to Donaldo Macedo's "Re-Inventing Paulo Freire Ethically"

CATHERY YEH

IN THE ERA OF Trump, Paulo Freire's ideas and ideals remained a light in the darkness. While systems of oppression and injustice have always existed, Trump's presidency marked a different type of social and political arrangement. Trump's anti-Black, anti-immigration, Islamophobic, and anti-feminist notions of "Making America Great Again" were adaptive and flexible manifestations of capitalism and White supremacy. This paper constitutes a personal response about the significance of Paulo Freire and Donaldo Macedo's work today, specifically for new scholars entering the academy. I build on the case for ethics and love as a powerful force for resistance within academia and with communities. I propose that revolutionary love serves as a moral and strategic compass for individual and collective action for transformative change. I begin with a recounting of my early exchanges with Paulo Freire's text as a young teacher and continue on to highlight current exchanges with Donaldo Macedo and the Paulo Freire Democratic Project in order to situate revolutionary love as emotion and praxis, both of which are relational and political.

Teaching as an Act of Love

I was introduced to Paulo Freire as a new teacher twenty years ago. *Pedagogy of the Oppressed* (1970), *Teachers as Cultural Workers: Letters to Those Who Dare to Teach* (1998a), and *Pedagogy of Freedom* (1998b) greatly shaped my view of teaching as a political project and one grounded in love. It was through Paulo Freire that I learned how to love as a teacher. It was love with its spontaneity and passion that gave me the strength and humility to work with my students and their families. I learned to challenge my own complacency and engage with them in critical literacies that opened our eyes and minds to the world's inequities, as well as its possibilities. My students invited me, a classroom teacher, into their homes, and these visits continued throughout my year as their teacher. Many still visit me today. It was through dialogue and collective unlearning and relearning inside the classroom walls and beyond that allowed the students and me to dream, to speak out, and to take action.

Ethics and Love Lost in the Academy and Beyond

Today, as a newly minted woman of color in the academy, Paulo Freire's ideas and ideals take on deeper meaning for me. Just a few years back as a graduate student, a senior faculty member of color advised me after a research presentation to "tone down my passion and to speak with less emotion" so that "my work would be seen with more credibility." His comment was just the first of many explicit reminders that the institution honors intellectuals who are seen as rational, pragmatic, and objective. However, Ana Maria Araújo ("Nita") Freire (2016) reminds us that "pragmatics is beholden to a capitalist market economy" (para. 20). Institutions fill an important niche in the reproduction of our capitalist society by equipping the population with the knowledge, values, and practices of a compliant workforce. We, as faculty members of these institutions in the postindustrial era, serve as machines for capitalist accumulation and are rewarded for our flexibility, competitiveness, economic rationale, and emotional detachment. This detachment leads to a perpetuation of *colonial scholarship* that exploits and dehumanizes children and communities in the name of *careerist* gains.

We are asked to sell our souls based on reward systems that require compliance and obedience to the *ethics of the market* using superficial competencies and measurable behaviors—numerical scores on student evaluations, impact factors of publications, citations, and awards—embedded in cultural repertoires and histories of racism and exclusion that ignore the diverse ways of being and knowing that women and folx of color bring to schools and the academy (Darder, 2017; hooks, 1994).

The university only mirrors, in its functioning, the ordering logics of the broader society. We live in a time of obscene greed and perverse consumerism. The United Nations figures that some 345 individuals—not companies—collectively enjoy wealth equivalent to the domestic product of 40% of poor countries (United Nations, 2013). When this data is shared with colleagues and friends, no one seems surprised. Such extreme inequities are seen as normal and unavoidable. In the era of Trump and global fascism, the *ethics of humanity* was clearly not a priority. Many would argue that it has never been one. We spend more money putting our youth behind bars than behind desks. In the past four decades, our U.S prison population has more than quadrupled; we now have the highest prison population in the world. More African Americans are under correctional control in prison or jail, on probation or parole, than were enslaved in 1850, a decade before the Civil War began (Alexander & West, 2012). We are living in a crisis of humanity in a society of mass incarceration.

In my own community of Los Alamitos, California, a Washington, DC-based hate group, Federation for American Immigration Reform (FAIR), engineered an orchestrated campaign against Senate Bill 54, the VALUES Act. California's VALUES Act is the strongest anti-Trump, pro-sanctuary law to date in the country. The law ensured that state resources were not used to fund mass deportation, and it offered protection for immigrant families. From the far-away swamp in DC, Los Alamitos and Orange County seemed like easy targets for FAIR to dismantle the fundamental provisions of California's VALUES Act.

White supremacy has a legacy in Orange County. Just a decade back, White residents made up the majority of the population. Henry W. Head, a prominent member of the Ku Klux Klan, was instrumental in Orange County's secession from Los Angeles County. Klan members, as well as members of other White nationalist groups like Native Sons and the John Birch Society, have served and continue to serve as elected city officials. With the backing of and funding from these local high-ranking officials, hate groups, 24/7 coverage by Fox News, and tweets by Trump himself, Los Alamitos, with a population smaller than most California high schools, became an anti-sanctuary city and set off the wave of anti-immigrant, anti-homeless, and anti-LGBTQIA policies and initiatives throughout the Southern California Coast.

In the last ten years, the demographics of Orange County have changed. No longer predominantly White, one-third of Orange County's residents are immigrants, and over half are folx of color. Therefore, the newly passed anti-sanctuary ordinance, promoted by FAIR, allowed ICE and local law enforcement to chase families out of places once considered to be sanctuaries. Homes, schools, hospitals, and courthouses no longer provided safe haven. In the era of Trump, people and children were disposable and blameworthy. Within my community, what was even more painful was the immobilizing ideology of fatalism that seemed to engulf families once the VALUES Act was dismantled. It seemed the U.S. empire was unraveling, and the American pursuit of unlimited economic growth had reached its social and ecological limits.

Grounded in identity politics, people were and are positioned against each other without realizing that class relations and the accumulation of capital are at the heart of global concerns. These capitalist relations were also at the heart of my city's immigration battle. Trump's reign built upon a legacy of capitalism in which large corporations and rich individuals used their power to ensure that policy works in their interest.

Ethics and Love as Resistance

I have reflected on Paulo Freire's life work and Donaldo Macedo's loyal and deep commitment to spreading and reinventing Freire's work for some time now. With every reflection of their shared ideals, I am brought back to the role of ethics and love as central to building resistance and in countering the domesticating powers of greed and violence in our society. Let me share a particular example from my own experience.

My last visit with Donaldo Macedo occurred in New York, the morning after the American Educational Research Association's (AERA) celebration of the 50th anniversary of *Pedagogy of the Oppressed*. We met at his hotel lobby and walked through the windy streets of Manhattan mostly in silence, until we arrived at a small deli for breakfast. As soon as we were given a table, Donaldo looked at me and spoke in his knowing way, "You may be smiling, but I can see pain behind that smile. It's in your eyes." At that moment, I started to cry.

During that breakfast, I was reminded that the road to making the world "more just, less dehumanizing, and more humane" requires a "developed coherence between words, actions, and ideas" (Macedo, 2021). I became keenly aware that the world often functions to disable our hearts, minds, and bodies. Coherence requires grounding our lives, not just our work, in seeing humanity in ourselves and in others.

Donaldo Macedo (2014), in a talk delivered at Loyola Marymount University, called for teachers to "unapologetically embrace the pedagogical principles developed by Paulo Freire" through "a revolutionary love infused with 'just ire,' compassion, passion, and an unyielding hope." Freire fervently argued that "we must do all things with feelings, dreams, wishes, fear, doubts, and passion" (Darder, 2017, p. 11). We should feel grief, disappointment, and be "justly angry" at the increasing exploitation, violence, and dehumanization seen and experienced within my community, at institutions, and around the world.

Nita Freire (2016), in her recent keynote speech celebrating the 50th anniversary of *Pedagogy of the Oppressed* at AERA in Washington, DC shared that Paulo Freire used to say:

> I do not know only by using my head, or only by using my intelligence. My knowledge comes from the confluence of things emanating from my whole body, without compartmentalization. It originates from the emotions, feelings and other sentiments that go through my body, and because of my body, and because of my mind. My body tells me about what I must reflect. It is my body that becomes restless, that mobilizes me for the search of knowledge.

Now, as a faculty member, it has been only from the privilege of sharing Paulo Freire's ideas and ideals in a variety of activities and through deeply humane professional and personal conversations with Donaldo Macedo and the Paulo Freire Democratic Project—Peter McLaren, Suzi SooHoo, Lilia Monzó, Anaida Colón-Muñiz, Miguel Zavala, and Jorge Rodriquez—that I am able to deepen my own understanding of the radical interconnectedness and spirituality in Paulo Freire's work. It is this spirituality, grounded in unwavering love and hope of *history as possibility*, that counters the dominating culture of individualism, materialism, and fatalism that drives our world. Paulo's life history reminds us that movements are born of critical connections and critical consciousness grounded in a political and radicalized form of love.

Love as Praxis

> *"This capacity to always begin anew, to make, to reconstruct, and to not spoil, to refuse to bureaucratize the mind, to understand and to live [life] as a process—live to become—is something that always accompanied me throughout life. That is an indispensable quality of a good teacher."*
>
> —Paulo Freire, 1993, p. 98

Within the last two years, I have witnessed two very different visions of my own community, one motivated by fear and despicable contempt for immigrants, and another grounded in humanity, a love for people and community. The anti-sanctuary actions opposing the California VALUES Act in Los Alamitos stirred up an anti-immigrant frenzy at city council meetings throughout the county. At council meetings, White nationalists descended with bullhorns and hate speech. Meanwhile, immigrant families, youth, and White allies countered hate with songs, stories about the immigrant experience, Korean drumming, and cumbia dancing.

Defiance of neoliberalism is often captured in global media through sound bites: the Martin Luther King, Jr.-and-Rosa Parks narrative or isolated large-scale marches (Purcell, 2016). Freire (1997), hooks (1994), and Boggs (2012) would argue that it is not one-time events or individual heroes that create social movements, but the everyday acts of resistance we all can engage in—as parents and children, as academics and artists, as teachers and students, as preachers and scientists—in which we have the ability and responsibility to break with market logic and to bring humanity back to the world.

In *Pedagogy of the Heart* (1997), Paulo Freire highlights the historical process needed to take place in schools and communities as anchored in relationships of solidarity. To challenge the individualist strains of the current ideology, we regain our own humanity through engagement with community. When the Los Alamitos City Council voted to opt out of the VALUES Act in order to become an "anti-sanctuary city," my family, our neighbors, teachers, and youth came together in partnership with the American Civil Liberties Union to sue our city the next day.

Each day, I am witnessing the power of collective humanity in creating change. I see families and children in my community speaking up inside the chamber walls of the city council and protesting in the streets. Mothers and teachers are gathering late at night after putting their children to bed. They are strategizing to reinvent school curricula. Teachers, students, and parents gather for weekly meetings and workshops to engage in dialectical thinking and action. Their mission is to enhance individual and collective agency on issues of healthcare, ethnic studies, and immigrant, LGBTQIA, and labor rights. These critical networks have been central to our weeding through and naming multiple and interlocking systems of oppression, and through praxis—the authentic union of action and reflection—we're working to re-make a new culture both as a site for the integration of community change and for the development of critical consciousness.

In contrast to my sense of belonging in community work, I struggle to find a place for myself in the academy. As academics, we are often forced "to engage in the social construction of not seeing" (Macedo, 2005, pp. 24-25) and rewarded for *being on our knees* to an institution that rewards deficit-based ideologies of students, neoliberal framings of the *problem*, individualism and competition, blinding us from seeing the power of building relationships and working together.

Just like movement building, it is only in and through communion with scholars like Donaldo Macedo, the Paulo Freire Democratic Project, and with my own children, students, and the community, that I have been helped to become more whole as a human being. They help me to question my ideological beliefs and intentions, to identify compliance in the academy by recognizing that every prescribed behavior to colonialism and careerism "moves my consciousness away from what I experience in the flesh to false abstracted reality and false understandings" (Darder, 2017, p. 41) of myself, my students, and our world.

I am learning to rediscover the nonmaterial things that bring me the greatest joy and fulfillment. I am learning to savor every minute of time with my eleven- and seven-year old. I recently developed a habit of spending a few minutes each night watching their sweet faces as they sleep. I try to sit next to and not across from my partner when we're at restaurants, something we didn't do even when we first dated. On rainy days, I often stop my trek to park on the side of the road, just for a few minutes, to enjoy the lulling sound of water drops tapping on the car windshield. It is through moments of joy, wonder, fear, anger, and hope in the world that allows me to be able to identify the forces that challenge our humanity and to see the historical possibilities for a more just and humane world.

References

Alexander, M., & West, C. (2012). *The new Jim Crow: Mass incarceration in the age of colorblindness.* The New Press.

Boggs, G.L. (2012). *The next American revolution: Sustaining activism for the twenty-first century.* University of California Press.

Darder, A. (2017). *Reinventing Paulo Freire: A pedagogy of love.* Routledge.

Freire, A.M.A. (2016). Critical pedagogy as an act of faith, love, and courage, presented at Cátedra Paulo Freire, Evanston, IL.

Freire, P. (1970). *Pedagogy of the oppressed.* Continuum.

Freire, P. (1993). *Pedagogy of the city.* Continuum.

Freire, P. (1997). *Pedagogy of the heart.* Continuum.

Freire, P. (1998a). *Teachers as cultural workers: Letters to those who dare to teach.* Westview.

Freire, P. (1998b). *Pedagogy of freedom: Ethics, democracy and civic courage.* Rowman & Littlefield.

hooks, b. (1994). *Teaching to transgress: Education for the practice of freedom.* Routledge.

Macedo, D. (2005). Introduction. In P. Freire, *Pedagogy of the Oppressed* (30th anniversary edition.). (pp. 11-28). Continuum.

Macedo, D. (2014, February 19). *The ethics of linguistic democracy in schools and society.* [Paper presentation]. Loyola Marymount University 2014 Leavy Presidential Chair Lecture, Los Angeles, CA, United States.

Macedo, D. (2021). Re-inventing Paulo Freire ethnically (Chapter Thirteen in the present volume). Myers Education Press.

Purcell, M. (2016). For democracy: Planning and publics without the state. *Planning Theory*, 15(4), 386–401.

United Nations. (2013) *Inequality Matters: Report of the World Social Situation 2013.* New York, NY: Author. https://www.un.org/esa/socdev/documents/reports/InequalityMatters.pdf

CHAPTER FIFTEEN

A Journey Toward Coherence: Responding to Donaldo Macedo

CHRISTIAN ALEJANDRO BRACHO

IN "RE-INVENTING PAULO FREIRE Ethically" (Chapter Thirteen in the present volume), Donaldo Macedo (2021) emphasizes that critical educators must "walk the walk" through political and intellectual coherence and warns that a failure to do so reproduces coloniality and deepens social injustices and inequities. Macedo draws on Freire to advise scholars and educators that they must get rid of the "gloves and masks" to meaningfully engage the world, drawing on "just anger" to re-invent Freirean ideals for new contexts and circumstances. Macedo (Chapter Thirteen herein) writes: "Today's unsettling landscape of ever-increasing misery and exploitation demands a careful consideration of the related consequences of different kinds of scholarship and pedagogy, of their ability to foster or forestall oppression."

Reading his chapter shook me, as I reflected on my own experiences as a teacher, activist, and scholar. *Do I cohere?* I wondered. As a teacher educator and scholar, do I meaningfully engage the world and cultivate experiences that allow teacher candidates to do the same, that is, "walk the walk?" Reflecting on these questions, I considered my time at the University of La Verne, a Hispanic Serving Institution in southern California. In recalling some of my experiences, my aim is to name a critical educational philosophy and demonstrate how teacher educators can cultivate coherence with it by walking the walk in their teaching and service. Then we can start the process that Macedo calls us to: "installing redressive measures to support the success of all youth."

Philosophical Coherence

I joined the teacher education program at the University of La Verne in August 2017. I had just moved back to California from Washington, D.C., where I worked in an international education program, primarily teaching courses about global educational issues. Moving into the Teacher Education Program at La Verne felt like a return home, given that I had spent ten years as a high school English teacher and teacher trainer in a local district. My arrival coincided with a program overhaul that would meet new standards, integrate new teacher dispositions, and include updated course content to reflect commitments to equity. Walking into this endeavor, I quickly realized I did not have a clear framework for thinking about my work as a teacher educator. What beliefs would I operate from? What actions would matter most to me, and align with my values?

Fortunately, my first days on the job were at a workshop with the teacher education faculty and Dr. Etta Hollins, teacher educator and author of *Transforming Culture for a Culturally Diverse Society* (1996). Dr. Hollins asked us to consider important questions as we moved forward with our new program, and asked the faculty to self-reflect on our program's philosophy. *What is our approach to teaching and learning? What do we do that is unique and special to us?* Listening to my new colleagues, I was struck by their thoughtful responses. They identified humanistic commitments to students' well-being, as well as a constructivist approach in the classroom.

Dr. Hollins encouraged us to explore these elements together. Over the course of several months, I worked with a group of faculty to develop a philosophy we called *humanistic constructivism*. We explained humanistic constructivism as valuing the individual experiences of learners while also paying close attention to the social context in which learners meet to make meaning of things. We described this approach to humanistic activities like reflective practice, experiential learning, and inquiry to the co-construction of knowledge through peer interaction. Our conclusion was that humanistic constructivism, as a philosophical framework in our program, favors the whole person, promotes choice and discovery, and utilizes a dialectical approach grounded in relationality and empathy. Such an approach, of course, can run counter to the neoliberal elements of a teacher education program, such as adherence to state credentialing standards, the realities of testing regimes that can create barriers to certification, and the economic strains that teacher candidates sometimes endure as they pursue the career, while also working part- or full-time jobs and raising families.

As a faculty, we worked hard to incorporate curriculum and assessments that walked the humanistic constructivism walk, in ways that would simultaneously prepare our teachers to successfully clear the professionalization hurdles ahead. Our core courses emphasized social and ethical ways of knowing: the power of relationships; the importance of interaction as a vehicle for knowing oneself, others, and the world; and the funds of knowledge students bring with them to the classroom.

In the course of my first year at La Verne, as I thought more carefully about humanistic constructivism, I realized that being in a teacher education program re-activated in me my identity as a teacher rather than as a professor. I observed how important it was for me to walk the walk as a *teacher*, to be, as Macedo (2021) says, *coherent* in how I modeled that role. I was reminded of Freire's (1998) assertion in *Teachers as Cultural Workers* that teachers must possess the quality of *lovingness*, "not only toward the students but also the very process of teaching," and mobilize it as *armed love*: "the fighting love of those convinced of the right and the duty to fight, to denounce, and to announce" (p. 40). As I ended my first year, I felt firmly grounded in a belief that I had come to a university where I could truly embrace my love for the teaching profession. In taking on the role of Co-Director of our college's Center for Educational Equity and Intercultural Research (CEEIR), I could also fight for equity and social justice.

Pedagogical Coherence

The summer after my first year, I attended a teacher educator fellowship at Arcadia University. One of my projects was to create a new syllabus for the Foundations of Education course I taught. Instinctually, I knew that *Pedagogy of the Oppressed* (Freire, 1970) needed to be included. Though I had read the text several times before, as an undergrad, master's student, and doctoral candidate, I had never taught the book. I was excited to bring Freire into the lives of my students but was not sure how I would help them unpack the text for its rich wisdom. Even in the fall, as the Freire session approached, I was stumped about what I would actually do in class. I lacked clarity on what I wanted students to experience, or what they should take away from the book. Re-reading the text in preparation, I was unexpectedly overwhelmed by the philosophical concepts that drove the first few chapters. I had previously read the book as a student of social movements and popular education, but I had not considered how it might be taught in a teacher education class. I wondered: How would I make the text coherent to my students?

The day of class, I sat in my office, flipping through the chapters again, hoping for a lesson idea to emerge. My attention turned to which words I had highlighted or underlined, and I remembered Freire's focus on literacy as reading the word *and* reading the world, and his assertion that the teacher is also a learner. Suddenly, a lesson began to take shape. I realized that to make the book coherent, I needed to be coherent with my practices, drawing on humanism and constructivism to engage *with* students to make sense of the book together. By showing students that I was also seeking to learn, we could embark on a quest for mutual humanization.

The lesson began with six words that I highlighted in the first few chapters: *ontology*, *axiology*, *conscientization*, *praxis*, *dialectical*, and *humanism*. I felt they were foundational to an understanding of the *Pedagogy of the Oppressed*. They would be our guiding stars—words that would initiate our examination of a problem-posing pedagogy and help define a path on which we could walk the walk together. I created a slide with the six words, printed a document with some key passages, and walked into class that evening not knowing how things would go.

I began class by foregoing any overview of an agenda or objectives, noting out loud that I felt doing so would be counter to Freire's vision. "Today let's figure this out together," I said, letting go of the feeling that I had to couch the learning in some special purpose or outcome. Instead, students randomized into four new groups, and each was tasked with unpacking one of the key words. As they discussed, I realized I had never made much use of the whiteboards that were on three of the four walls, so I improvised: each group would brainstorm on the boards, providing definition and context for how the words were used in Freire's text.

The first group was assigned ontology, and they defined it as a "theory of existence." The group described how traditional models of education prohibit students from ontological exploration, i.e., from looking at the world around them rather than the textbook in front of them. The second group explored axiology, and they defined it as the "study of what makes things valuable or ethical." The group argued that Freire's vision of pedagogy is more ethical because it values what learners already bring to the table and compels people to pose questions about the world. The third group defined praxis as "proactive practice" and drew a visual that demonstrated this cycle within a problem-posing pedagogy. The fourth group defined humanism as "a belief in the power and potential of human beings" and claimed that the banking model of education was anti-humanist because, as Freire (1970) wrote, it "fails to acknowledge men and women as historical beings" (p. 84). One group then went on to examine dialectic, and drew an image that showed a conversational exchange between two talking heads, with arrows that illustrated the "thesis-antithesis-synthesis" that comes from a meaningful exchange of ideas. Another group took on conscientization and used a definition they found online: "the process of developing critical awareness of one's social reality through praxis." Their notes linked the term to a problem-posing pedagogy that seeks liberation and thrives on creativity. Students had the chance to travel to other groups and examine their brainstorms, adding words, ideas, and images with their markers as they annotated and made sense of each other's work.

As the students discussed the words, drew their images, and admired each other's processes, I was struck by the mood in the room. Though we'd enjoyed our time together in the course of the semester, the sense of light and wonder was now palpable. There was something liberating about defining words for ourselves, about being tentative in our conceptualizations rather than seeking affirmation or external validation. Using the whiteboards also made the activity feel malleable: words or ideas could be erased as the ideas became refined. We were at once humanizing ourselves, and each other, while also constructing knowledge. We were using our social bonds as students to know the world and "do" the learning, but also drawing on our various cognitive, artistic, and moral capacities to create knowledge in ways that were unique to ourselves, our context, and our desires.

After the initial vocabulary activity, we decided it was a good time for close reading. We read the text aloud and talked about how our initial grounding in key concepts helped us make better sense of Freire's words. Students described how the ontological and axiological dimensions of the text surfaced once they had a better comprehension of what those words meant. They explained that the text took on a more urgent tone, since they now understood *Pedagogy of the Oppressed* as grounded in existential and ethical questions about being in and knowing the world. We also discussed the challenges of such an approach within the standards-based models of schooling that currently dominate public education in the United States. We wondered aloud whether teaching in our country can meaningfully be transformed into a problem-posing model. Some students argued that Common Core State Standards reforms push for greater critical thinking and creativity, but found that many teachers preferred older rote models that maintained the teacher-student hierarchy surrounding who has knowledge and who receives it.

Following our discussion, we had different questions or interests, so we decided to move into an inquiry mode, where each of us could take some individual time to research or reflect. We gave ourselves 20 minutes, during which time some explored the idea of critical pedagogy in their respective fields of math, science, language arts, social studies, or physical education, while others learned more about Freire from videos or websites. The quiet time to explore our own interests offered a good opportunity for individual introspection after a sustained period of group work and dialogue. During this time I wondered what might be a good way to wrap up the class, and remembered Augusto Boal's (1993) *Theatre of the Oppressed*. Though I was not versed in Boal's techniques, I thought students using their bodies to bring Freire's ideas or concepts to life could prove valuable.

After debriefing our individual inquiry time, I asked groups to select any idea from *Pedagogy of the Oppressed* and dramatize it using a short skit. Students quickly organized and used their creativity to construct their story or frame. One group selected the "banking model of education" and used a repetitive action, with one individual handing another (a teacher) a piece of paper and cash; the middle person then handed the paper to the third person (a student) while holding fast to the money. Another group had a student stand in the middle of a circle with her eyes closed and covered by her hands. She asked questions out loud as individuals traveled around her in a circle, offering images and insights on pieces of paper, which the student could not see because she was "closed off ontologically." The mood was light and jovial as we played with these concepts in ways that were humanizing to all.

Following our skits, we used a restorative circle to discuss what we had just experienced. We felt a sense of creative energy, a spark, that had been generated through the initial vocabulary activity and carried throughout the three hours. One student said she finally understood Freire and felt empowered to employ a problem-posing approach to her math classes. Another student explained how he would use a humanizing approach in his physical education classes, where students often feel dehumanized by the competitive aspects of the games. We all felt that Freire encouraged us to "walk the walk" of being humanizing educators who valued the knowledge and experiences of our students, who we would see as partners in dialogue, rather than the recipients of our teaching. We had sought coherence—and achieved it together.

Professional Coherence

Later that year, in my role as CEEIR Co-Director, I worked to bring critical pedagogy into the lives of our students and to the community at large. Inspired by the work of the Paulo Freire Democratic Project, CEEIR decided to hold a one-day conference in March 2019 entitled "Critical Pedagogy in the 21st Century." The conference asked: Given Jair Bolsonaro's efforts to erase Paulo Freire's legacy in Brazil, *how will critical pedagogy continue to thrive*? When we selected the dates of the conference, we could not have predicted that in the days and weeks prior to the event, our campus would be torn apart by hate crimes and racial tension.

As a minority-serving institution, the university had been grappling with what it means to actually *serve* minority students, rather than simply enroll them. This question became more prominent following student protests in Fall 2018 that called for inclusive faculty hiring, more culturally relevant pedagogies, and diversity training for staff and faculty. The student protests revealed a long-held feeling that the university—in its curriculum, pedagogy, or practices—did not reflect the diversity of the students.

The day before our March conference, the campus was shocked by reports that a student's car had been set ablaze in apparent retaliation for the student's involvement in the campus protests. Some students received social media messages with racial slurs and threats. The campus community was outraged. Students and faculty of color, in particular, felt a sense of "just anger," a term used by Macedo (see Chapter Thirteen in the present volume) and wondered how the university would respond. As event organizers, we felt compelled to reframe the conference as an opportunity for dialogue, reflection, and action. Over 120 people attended our morning session, and the Dean of the College of Education led the day with a powerful call for the community to come together and engage in much-needed reflection about racism and violence. More importantly, her message was that critical pedagogy is needed more than ever, as a means for praxis, conscientization, and transformation.

Over the course of the day—as we learned about critical pedagogy across the disciplines, about community praxis through dance, about critically mentoring youth of color, and about student activism and leadership—we discovered how we might get into the fight, taking off our "gloves and masks" (Macedo, Chapter Thirteen herein) in a battle to preserve and demand our humanity. Keynote speaker Peter McLaren offered a keen example of how to live in this manner, using illustrations of his own life's trajectory to show how, in each step we take, we can move toward coherence as educators, scholars, and activists.

What I learned from the conference was that CEEIR could facilitate coherence for the university by offering opportunities for people to "walk the walk" together. To that end, the Center hosted a Critical Education Forum in October 2019 with Dr. Gina Garcia, an expert on Hispanic Serving Institutions (HSIs). We invited her to campus to lead a full day of events aimed at helping the university understand what HSIs are and how they can actually serve the needs of Hispanic/Latinx students. Dr. Garcia's events offered various members of the community, such as students, staff, administrators, and faculty, the chance to understand how being culturally responsive and sustaining is an essential component of educational equity. One way in which CEEIR manifested this vision was by creating two new undergraduate courses entitled *Critical Pedagogies* and *Neurodiversity*. We also began to work with stakeholders to design a potential Critical Pedagogy Studies major. Through these efforts, I have sought to bring Freire's notions of lovingness and armed love into my work outside the classroom, cohering these two aspects of my work.

Self-Reflection

I am a gay, Latinx cisgender male, born to Mexican immigrants who came to Los Angeles in the 1970s. My journey has taken me across the country several times to be educated and to work in institutions of higher learning. It is only now, at a Hispanic Serving Institution, that I realize how my identity was fragmented as I tried to do my work at other universities. At La

Verne, I feel a tangible coherence as the line between my personal and professional identities fades, as I see my own personal struggles and beliefs aligning with the work ahead of me. I embrace Freire's humanism and refuse to use my work as an opportunity, as Donaldo Macedo puts it in Chapter Thirteen of the present volume, "to further the researcher's own crass careerist interests." I am not interested in furthering my career in the academy. Instead, my aim is to walk the walk as a partner with my colleagues, as a teacher-student in my classes, and as an empowered member of the world community, driven by just anger and equipped with armed love to create change.

References

Boal, A. (1998). *Threat of the oppressed*. Theater Communications Group.
Freire, P. (1970). *Pedagogy of the oppressed*. Continuum.
Freire, P. (1998). *Teachers as cultural workers: Letters to those who dare teach*. Westview Press.
Hollins, E.R. (1996). *Transforming culture for a culturally diverse society*. Routledge.
Macedo, D. (2021). Re-inventing Paulo Freire ethically. In C. Achieng-Evensen, K. Stockbridge, & S. SooHoo (Eds.), *Freirean echoes: Scholars and practitioners dialogue on critical ideas in education* (pp ??–??). Myers Education Press.

Section Five: Questions and Activity

Question

1. In Macedo's chapter, he addresses the ways in which neoliberalism creates mania around productivity and perpetuates careerist orientations in higher education. What effect does the specter of neoliberalism have in the spaces in which you work? Are there means of confrontation, resistance, and survival? If so, what are they? In what ways do you or others confront, resist, or deal with these effects?
2. Using love as a moral compass, Yeh suggests that we reframe our responses to the oppressive conditions created by neoliberalism. In what ways does love reveal itself in your practices?
3. Bracho draws us into his journey toward an integrated, anti-neoliberal intellectual, pedagogical, and activist coherence. How does he define coherence? Is there coherence among your beliefs, curricula, and activism?

Activity: Naming Exercise

The readings in this section reveal the importance of awareness of and responses to the influence of neoliberalism in our lives. In the next week, make a list of the influences in curriculum, policies, hierarchies, governance, human relations, etc., that show how neoliberalism is at play in your institution. After doing this, take some time to reflect on what helps you and others to deal with, resist, or subvert neoliberal forces. This could be a conceptual framework, a list of practices, or new wisdom or insights.

AFTERWORD

A Meditative Breath

Suzanne SooHoo, Kevin Stockbridge, & Charlotte Achieng-Evensen

"One of us tells a dream and we breathe life into it."
—Wheatley, 2001, p. 43

This quote captures the poetic life force of this book. We conceived of dreaming as purposeful imagining, "a word-action implying praxis" (A. Freire, Chapter One herein)—as Nita Freire would state it: untested feasibility. Dreaming provides opportunities for reconceptualizing our world in ways that are both collaborative and inclusive. Dreaming allows for us to engage in praxis that is humanizing. As we dream together, we breathe life into the dream. Our togetherness has the ability to transform the ideological and experiential actions we take in the world. This text includes many breaths—the many ways in which we, as a community of authors, gathered to re-imagine how Freirean thoughts echo within our varying contexts. The story of this book highlights the ways those authors breathed life into these ideas.

The first living breath of this text took place at a historical moment. It was a coming together of approximately 300 scholars and activists to rededicate the Paulo Freire Critical Pedagogy Archives at the Leatherby Libraries at Chapman University (https://tinyurl.com/FreireArchives). At the symposium, distinguished scholars spoke of Paulo's influence on their lives. Recognizing the potential impact of these speeches, we, the editors, breathed a second breath into this dream. We assembled a text that could immortalize the moment. From its genesis, *Freirean Echoes: Multigenerational Dialogues in Contemporary Times* was a conversational book—a text in which the initial speeches of distinguished scholars were dialogically positioned with the responses of others. Each section is centered on an original speech. Within the section, two additional authors breathe new life into the initial ideas, transferring their energies in the form of dialogic reverberations and amplifications. Thus, the structure of the book evolved into five sections housing dialogic communities of authors.

As the book moved through its various constructions, we added section questions and activities to expand the dialogic space and to bring theory into practice. This afterword is an essential part of the book as it invites you, the reader, to breathe life into these ideas. Your active engagement with this text moves this dialogue forward into the present moment and into your own context. As editors, we note that this sharing of air and relational discourse takes on the form of an intentional community.

We wonder how you will breathe life into the dreams and challenges taking shape in our current moment. For us, Wheatley's poetic phrase has become a mantra. What follows are some of the ways that we are in an active *dream-imagination* state, breathing life into ideas and pondering what might take shape.

"One of us tells a dream and we breathe life into it."

—Wheatley, 2001, p. 43

Dialogue and Lockdown

Dialogue is communal (Darder, 2018). In *Freirean Echoes: Multigenerational Dialogues in Contemporary Times*, the intentionality of linking together designated readers created a momentary space of belonging. As a reader, I am invited into this reader-response space to breathe air, generating new life. I am not alone because I have touched, and been touched by the words of each author. We are, collectively, life givers to the initial chapter. These cooperative engagements are comforting during the pandemic. To enter a portal of an intellectual community where ideas breathe air without ventilators, masks, or social distancing mandates, I am invigorated and temporarily freed from the weight of the multiple layers of lethargy, depression, fatigue, and social alienation I have felt during the pandemic lockdown. It is not a good substitute for genuine people, but it is a worthy surrogate.

"One of us tells a dream and we breathe life into it."

—Wheatley, 2001, p. 43

Dialogue and Racism

Which will kill us first? Covid-19 or racism? We are racing for a cure for both. Or are we? Can we be vaccinated and protected from White supremacy? Among the social "texts" of this moment—"Black Lives Matter," "I can't breathe," "Stop Asian Hate"—racism's persistence is disheartening, especially in our current state of vulnerability. This omnipotent virus can wipe out lives, but racism prevails, continuing to kill and compromise the spirit of living beings.

It is not enough *not* to be racist; rather, one should transcend entrenched systems and be anti-racist (Kendi, 2019). It is not simply a matter of doing no harm; it is a moral mandate to advance the good. We advocate for the social, economic, and physical well-being of all people; someone who works toward dismantling institutionalized inequities. This means naming and reforming those social structures embedded with racial injustice in all its multiple forms—poverty, police brutality, education, housing, employment, and so forth.

Recently we have seen anti-racist reform in architectural and policy changes: statues taken down, buildings renamed, initiatives for defunding the police, formation of community oversight groups, to name but a few. There is also a visible rise in global consciousness of systemic racism—a transnational human rights movement. People have risked contracting the deadly Covid-19 virus to stand strong against racism. The concept of systemic racism appears to have gone mainstream. This transnational intersectionality reflects a meta-dialogue of sorts. Perhaps together we can breathe new life.

"One of us tells a dream and we breathe life into it."

—Wheatley, 2001, p. 43

Dialogue and Change

Dialogue helps us understand change. In a world where nothing stays the same (Greene, 1995), and where we ourselves are always changing, collaborative dialogic inquiry helps us handle the unexpected. Dialogue begins with two, and collective dialogue with three or more. Within the liminal space created by dialogue, we move from individual imperatives to collective responsibility. Together we work to transform systems in more inclusive ways. Dialogue, therefore, is an essential tool for social movements. Kumashiro (2020) speaks of the power of collective mobilization: "Social movements change policy and law, they transform institutions and social relations and the very conditions of life, and they do so through collective action to queer the ideas that have become normalized and commonsensical . . . " (p. 82).

From struggle, hope emerges. At the intersection of struggle and hope, collective dialogue releases the potential of freedom. In so doing, collective dialogue affirms that we are all on a journey in search of a social vision of a more humane, more fully pluralist, more just, and more joyful community (Greene, 61).

> *"One of us tells a dream and we breathe life into it."*
>
> —Wheatley, 2001, p. 43

References

Darder. A. (2018). *Student guide to Freire's Pedagogy of the oppressed.* Bloomsbury.

Freire, A. (2021).The presence of Paulo Freire at Chapman University. In C. Achieng-Evensen, K. Stockbridge, & S. SooHoo (Eds.), *Freirean echoes: Scholars and practitioners dialogue on critical ideas in education.* Myers Education Press.

Greene, M. (1995). *Releasing the imagination.* Wiley.

Kendi, I. (2019). *How to be an antiracist.* One World.

Kumashiro, K. (2020). *Surrendered: Why progressives are losing the biggest battles in education.* Teachers College Press.

Wheatley, M. (2001). *Turning to one another: Simple conversations to restore hope to the future.* Berrett-Koehler Publishers.

ABOUT THE AUTHORS

Charlotte Achieng-Evensen is a K-12 practitioner and academic. Currently, she serves her school district as a Teacher Specialist focusing on research, policy, program coordination, and instructional coaching. At the university level, Dr. Achieng-Evensen teaches a variety of courses in teacher education. Her scholarly work is centered in the intersections of Indigenous Philosophies and colonization, culturally responsive methodologies, and K-12 teaching praxis.

Christian Alejandro Bracho is an Associate Professor in the LaFetra College of Education at the University of La Verne, where he also serves as Associate Program Chair of Teacher Education and as a Faculty Diversity Liaison. His research focuses on teacher identity, teacher movements, and LGBTQ communities. Most recently, he is the co-editor of Teachers Teaching Nonviolence, a volume with narratives by 18 K-12 teachers bringing nonviolence education to their schools and communities all over the United States.

Anaida Colón-Muñiz is Professor Emeritus, Chapman University. She was a coordinator and taught in the Master of Arts in Teaching and PhD programs for Attallah College of Educational Studies. She served as director of community education at Centro Comunitario de Educación. Her research includes bilingual education, language policy, international education, critical multicultural teacher education, and civil rights in education. Her publications include *Memories of Paulo Freire* (2010) and *Latino Civil Rights in Education: La Lucha Sigue* (2016).

Antonia Darder is a distinguished international Freirean scholar, a public intellectual, educator, writer, activist, and artist. She holds the Leavey Presidential Endowed Chair of Ethics and Moral Leadership at Loyola Marymount University, Los Angeles and is Professor Emerita of Education Policy, Organization, and Leadership at the University of Illinois Urbana Champaign. She also holds a Distinguished Visiting faculty post at the University of Johannesburg, in South Africa.

Ana Maria Araújo Freire is a critical scholar from Brazil and the widow of Paulo Freire. She holds a doctorate from the Pontifícia Universidade Católica de São Paulo where she also served as a faculty member. She also holds a Doctor Honoris Causa from Universidade Federal de Mato Grosso do Sul in Brazil. Her work continues to extend the critical thought of her husband across the globe.

Petar Jandrić is Professor at the Zagreb University of Applied Sciences, Croatia, and visiting professor at the University of Wolverhampton, UK. His previous academic affiliations include Croatian Academic and Research Network, National e-Science Centre at the University of Edinburgh, Glasgow School of Art, and Cass School of Education at the University of East London. He is Editor-in-Chief of Postdigital Science and Education journal and book series. Personal website: http://petarjandric.com/.

Donaldo Macedo is a critical theorist, linguist, and expert on literacy and education studies. He is the founder and former chair of the Applied Linguistics Master of Arts Program at the University of Massachusetts Boston. Macedo has been a central figure in the field of critical pedagogy for more than 20 years. His work with Paulo Freire broke new theoretical ground, as it helped to develop a critical understanding of the ways in which language, power, and culture contribute to the positioning and formation of human experience and learning. Macedo was Freire's chief translator and English language interpreter.

Peter McLaren is Distinguished Professor in Critical Studies at Attallah College of Educational Studies, Chapman University and Chair Professor, Northeast Normal University, China. A political activist and award-winning author, he has published 50 books in the areas of political sociology of education, critical pedagogy and liberation theology.

Lilia D. Monzó is Associate Professor in the Attallah College of Educational Studies at Chapman University and Co-director of the Paulo Freire Democratic Project. She is the author of A Revolutionary Subject: Pedagogy of Women of Color and Indigeneity. Monzó teaches on social movements and history and philosophies of education.

Edgar Orejel is a K-12 queer critical educator of color who is engaged in the enduring process of decolonizing their mind, body and spirit. This work extends into all facets of their life, including the educational setting, because they believe the classroom has the potential to be a transformational space where youth can be inspired to become the best and most authentic versions of themselves. You can visit them at www.elprofesoreo.com.

Suzanne SooHoo is the former Endowed Hassinger Chair in Education and the co-director, emerita of the Paulo Freire Democratic Project at Chapman University, Orange, California. She is one of ten Asian American endowed chairs in the U.S. Her current research interests focuses on critical pedagogy, Freirean philosophy and culturally responsive methodologies. As a former school principal and full professor, she has committed a lifetime to understanding and nurturing relationships and engaging dialogically towards the development of a more humane and socially just world.

Kevin Stockbridge is an Assistant Professor and Student Affairs Liaison in the Master of Arts in Teaching program at Chapman University. He is a critical educator and researcher dedicated to a radically inclusive world through engagement of democracy in the classroom and beyond. Kevin has co-edited and co-authored with scholars on several works that seek to advance and reframes transformative educational conversations for the sake of social justice.

Gregory Warren wrote his dissertation on Democratic Leadership Development in City Government. Upon completion of this project renewed his commitment to teach as a member of the Leadership Studies faculty at Chapman University. As a Freirean Scholar with the Paulo Freire Democratic Project, Greg is involved with research and writing serve engagement with the legacy and philosophical contributions of Paulo Freire. In additional to his service as a researcher and teacher, he recently founded Alchemy Associates.

Kimberly A. White-Smith is Professor and Dean of the LaFetra College of Education at the University of La Verne, an HSI serving 50% Latinx and 40% first-generation students. With over 25 years of urban schooling and educator development experience, Dr. White-Smith endeavors to foster academic justice for Black, Indigenous, Queer, Latinx, and neurodivergent students through enhanced learning environments, policies, and practices. She's authored publications on teacher and student learning, equity, leadership, and currently Black Mother-Scholars.

Tom Wilson was the co-founding director the Paulo Freire Democratic Project at Chapman University. He acquired Paulo's blessing to start the project through a simple handshake agreement. Tom's devoted colleagues and students are among the authors in this book. He died December 2018. This book is dedicated to Tom, good friend, intellectual, activist, lover of humanity.

Cathery Yeh is an assistant professor of mathematics education and the founding co-director of the Ethnic Studies Program at Chapman University. With 20+ years in education, beginning her tenure as a bilingual teacher in Los Angeles and abroad in China, Chile, Peru and Costa Rica, Cathery visited over 300 student homes and integrated students' lived experiences, knowledge and identities into the curriculum. Her research centers on critical mathematics education, humanizing practices, ethnic studies, and social justice teaching and organizing.

INDEX